TO WHOM IT MAY CONCERN

Tenets of the famous and the infamous

DOUG Mc PHILLIPS

Authors Other Visionary Stories:

From Darkness to Light
Awake to My Gutted Dream
The Sword of Discernment
Santiago Traveller
I' Prophet
Masters at my table
The Guru of Jerusalem
We Are Me Upside Down (Biography)
The Wicklow Way
The Adventures of Ace McDice,
Stretch Deed & Moonshine Melody
Instant Karma & Grace
The Credo
Reflections of an Old Man
A Writer on the Rocks
Reincarnation of the Assassin
Master of the Arts
Masters of Introspection
The Songs, not the Singer
Doug McPhillips July 2024

This book is copyrighted; apart from any fair dealing for private study, research, criticism or review, as permitted under the Copyright Act, no part may be reproduced by any process without the editor's written permission.

ISBN. 978-0-6486214-7-8 eBook 978-0-6486214-8-5

National Library of Australia Catalog- in -publication data:
Google research-Authors Unknown. Other references are at the back of this book.

This book is a work of fact, not fiction. All characters in this novel research reprints herein, and names of people living at the time may be fictitious. Any resemblance to actual events, locales, or persons living or dead is entirely coincidental but, where applicable, is real. Where poetic license is used to turn fact into fiction, names have been changed to protect the innocent.

Introduction:

In considering the world's political, economic and secular state in this 21st Century with all its pretence, drudgery and broken dreams, and with an eye to the spiritual, everything apart from a religious standpoint appears to be in a state of flux in the present day. Therefore it is hardly surprising that people seem lost and bewildered, overburdened by living a financial roller coaster, being bombarded with daily horrific news on the home front and internationally. Our media induces more fear of countable and unaccountable distractions for the populace in the domestic economy whilst bombarding graphic visual images of wars in play in the Middle East and Ukraine, street violence and political unrest at home and abroad.

The first world has gone mad with a lust for power, wealth and deeds of inhumanity to humankind that are more than ever prevalent in our society at large. Coupled with this state of affairs are the growing signs of mental disorders and the hospital system is overcrowded with patients who just can't cope. It is more a first-world problem where affluence and proof of worth are measured in dollars and cents, whilst those in poorer countries survive with little yet live out Christ's message of loaves and fishes. The idea of living in this world but not being of this world is foreign and somewhat unheard of in our society.

The measure of kindness, understanding, charity and giving to the poor is overridden by libertarianism, pride, greed, covertness, and lust for pleasurable pursuits to the detriment of the individual, the community and society. None of us are saints, but we have a duty of care for ourselves and our fellow man.

Is there an answer or semblance of hope in this world of deceit and lies in our world of artificial intelligence? Where is the truth now, and how does one find a way forward to live in this world for the better? To find this out and find a template for living a better life within the plan of natural order is what I seek to explore here. To move forward, it may be worthwhile to look back.

So, I have selected snippets of the philosophies from some of the famous and infamous people throughout history, writing a brief story about each of their lives, what they stood for and how they expressed their belief in a mission for the betterment or decrement of humanity. It is to be hoped that herein you, the reader, gain a template of ideas to utilise in daily life. Here, I hoped to capture the crux of the goal or aspirations from their creative works, philosophic utterances and mission statements in times of war as well as in times of peace to give the reader insight into a manual of guidance to improve our way of life in the service of all human beings for the greater good.

We must be enlightened to action for the well-being of humanity whilst we have the time. For one day, the 'bell will toll', and we will realise it also tolls for you and me.

Contents:

Chapter 1. Poet and Playwright. Page 7.

Chapter 2. A Man with a Mission. Page 17.

Chapter 3. Francis of Assisi. Page. 27.

Chapter 4. Mother Teresa of Calcutta. Page 35.

Chapter 5. A Message on Leadership. Page 41.

Chapter 6. Gandhi's protests and Speeches. Page 51.

Chapter 7. The King of Civil Rights. Page 59.

Chapter 8. The 'X' Factor. Page. 71.

Chapter 9. When the end game is a lie. Page 81.

Chapter 10. The Genius who tapped world Vibrations. Page. 91.

Chapter 11. The dangers of Indifference. Page. 103.

Chapter 12. In Conclusion. Page. 111.

"We cannot change what we are not aware of, and once we are aware, we cannot help but change."

Sheryl Sandberg

Lean In: Women, Work, and the Will to Lead (Goodreads)

CHAPTER 1.

POET AND PLAYWRIGHT

The lesson in this chapter is more about introspection on the need for change personally and the understanding of humanity's cry, too. It's a look into the philosophy of those who come to realise the meaning of life and the call to action before it's too late.

Dylan Thomas was one of the first relatively modern poets to realise all too late the reality of love and life as he contemplated death and looked back on life's lessons. He was born October 27, 1914, in Glamorgan, Wales and died November 9, 1953, in New York, U.S. He was a Welsh poet and prose writer whose work is known for its comic exuberance, rhapsodic lilt, and sadness His personal life, punctuated by reckless bouts of drinking, was well known whilst he suffered all his life from a lung condition and constant ill health, it did not stop his excessive smoking and drinking bouts.

Thomas spent his childhood in southwestern Wales. His father taught English at the Swansea grammar school, which the boy eventually attended. Dylan's mother was a farmer's daughter, so he had a country home he could visit on holiday.

Although he edited the school magazine and contributed poetry and prose to it, Thomas could have done better at school because he was intellectually lazy about subjects that did not directly concern him. His practical knowledge of English poetry, however, was enormous.

Thomas's first book, *18 Poems*, appeared in 1934, and it announced a strikingly new and individual, if not always comprehensible, voice in English poetry. His original style was further developed in *Twenty-Five Poems* (1936) and *The Map of Love* (1939). Thomas's work, in its overtly emotional impact, the importance of sound and rhythm, primitivism, and insistence on tensions between biblical echoes and sexual imagery, owed more to his Welsh background than to the prevailing taste in English literature for grim social commentary. Therein lay its originality. The poetry written up to 1939 concerns introspective, obsessive, sexual, and religious currents of feeling. Thomas seems to be arguing rhetorically with himself on the subjects of sex and death, character defects and redemption, the natural processes, creation and decay. The writing shows prodigious energy, but the final effect is sometimes obscure or diffuse.

Thomas made London his home for some ten years from about 1936. He had become famous in literary circles. In 1937, he married Caitlin McNamara, with whom he had two sons and a daughter. His attempts to make money with the BBC and as a film scriptwriter were not sufficiently remunerative, and the family was impoverished. He wrote film scripts during World War 11, having been excused from military service owing to a lung condition. Unfortunately, he was lacking in any sort of business acumen. He fell severely behind with his income tax returns, and what money he managed to make was taken from him, at source, by the British Exchequer. He took to drinking more heavily and borrowing from wealthier friends. Still, he continued to work, though, in his maturity, the composition of his poems became an ever-slower and more precise business.

The poems collected in Deaths and Entrances (1946) show a more extraordinary lucidity and confirm Thomas as a religious poet. This book reveals an advance in sympathy and understanding due, in part, to the impact of World War II and the deepening harmony between the poet and his Welsh background, for he writes generally in a mood of reconciliation and acceptance. He often adopts a bardic tone and is a true romantic in claiming a high, almost priestlike function for the poet. He also extensively uses Christian myth and symbols and often sounds a note of formal ritual and magic in his poems. The re-creation of childhood experience produces a visionary, mystical poetry in which the landscapes of youth and infancy assume the holiness of the first Eden ("Poem in October" "Fern Hill"); for Thomas, childhood, with its intimations of immortality, is a state of innocence and grace.

Whilst Thomas wrote numerous radio scripts, plays and books in his short life that we could use as a basis for a thesis on Dylan Thomas's work, our purpose here is different. Instead, I am drawn more to one poem suited to coming to grips with the meaning of life for thought-proving analysis for our mutual benefit in the telling.

The poem I write is " Do not go gently into that good night," for it sums up human misguidance in the focus on the material world as opposed to that of the spiritual path, in the biblical text and philosophy as the righteous path for all of humankind. Whilst academics presume a more abstract view of the poem, I believe it has a much deeper meaning than those expressed by the worldly-wise gentlemen of educated guessing. Firstly, let us look at the poem in its entirety.

Do not go gentle into that good night,
Old age should burn and rave at the close of day;
Rage, rage against the dying of the light.

Though wise men at their end know dark is right
Because their words had forked no lightning they,
Do not go gentle into that good night.

Good men, the last wave by, crying how bright
Their frail deeds might have danced in a green bay,
Rage, rage against the dying of the light.

Wild men who caught and sang the sun in flight,
And learn, too late, they grieved it on its way,
Do not go gentle into that good night.

Grave men, near death, who see with blinding sight
Blind eyes could blaze like meteors and be gay,
Rage, rage against the dying of the light.

And you, my father, there on the sad height,
Curse, bless me now with your fierce tears, I pray.
Do not go gentle into that good night.
Rage, rage against the dying of the light.

In "Do Not Go Gentle Into That Good Night," the poet acknowledges that death is inevitable everyone dies, sooner or later. But that doesn't mean that people should simply give up and give in to death. Instead, the speaker argues that people should fight fiercely and bravely against death. The mood of 'Do not go gentle into that good night' is sorrowful and solemn.

Dylan Thomas was undoubtedly reflecting on the meaning of his own life and wrote this poem as an object lesson for humanity.

So, in the poem's first line, the poet says that people shouldn't just give up when they face death; the speaker doesn't want them to be "gentle" about it. Instead, as He clarifies in the following two lines, he or she wants people to fight bravely and fiercely against death. Old people should "burn and rave" when they face death which the speaker calls "the close of the day" (using the same metaphor as the previous line: death is like darkness).

Thomas emphasises the passion he wants to see by using another metaphor: He wants us to understand that "old age should burn and rage' -" old people are as passionate as fire when they fight against death. Thomas tells them to "Rage against the dying of the light." The repetition of the word "rage" is an instance of the intensity that Thomas hopes to cultivate against death- through another metaphor that uses darkness and light: "the dying of the light."

The wise person "knows" that death is inevitable, but their failure to make a significant impact on the world through their words and actions leaves them unfulfilled, and they still fight against death. The phrase "forked no lightning" suggests that their words and actions did not have a powerful or lasting impact.

In these lines, the Poet describes how "good men" may feel that their "frail deeds" in life could have been more spectacular—so spectacular they may have "danced in a green bay." The Green Bay is a symbolic space that symbolises the time before "the last wave" had passed when the future was still "bright" with the promise of things to come for services to others. Still, life got in the way, and time ran out to do more good deeds as the afternoon emphasised death was on the horizon. They proclaim their works as good, but as Thomas goes on into the following line, "their frail deeds might have danced in a green bay," he laments the idea of a person knowing that their deeds will not be remembered regardless of how seemingly significant they were.

Similarly, the "wild men" the poet describes have spent their lives joyously and recklessly: they "caught and sang the sun in flight." But when they face death, they realise that they "grieved it on its way." In other words, they realise they regret the frivolous way they lived when it was too late.

The primary sentiment of "Do Not Go Gentle Into That Good Night" is that life is precious and should be fought for at every turn. The poem's speaker offers insight into how to face death with dignity and ferocity rather than resignation, believing that people should "burn and rave" as they approach death.

Then comes the finale. Thomas presents another oxymoron: "Curse, bless me now with your fierce tears." This refers to passionate tears as a blessing and a curse, which insinuates that Thomas does not necessarily believe death itself is inherently wrong, but to remain addresses the father, who seems to be on the verge of death. The speaker prays to be blessed and cursed by the father's tears. The tears are a blessing because they are "fierce," affirming life in the face of death. They're a curse because they signal the unyielding approach of death. Jesus, in his abandonment on the cross, cried out to The Father. It seems to me that the father, in this instance, was suffering the pain of the son as equally as the son suffered unto death.

So we need to view our lives and humanity in general, always mindful that we have but one day at a time to act mindfully, being as vigilant as a female serpent and gentle as a dove in all we see and do.

William Shakespeare was yet another of the poets and playwrights who recognised in "The Seven Ages of Man" the apparent distraction of life as we age has a progression but to what avail. So it is that I turned to write his brief Shakespeare, William.

Shakespeare's exact date of birth is unknown, but his baptism in Stratford Avon, in Warwickshire, on 26th April 1546, confirms he was born somewhere in that vicinity at that time. William's father, a man of some standing in the community, was sometimes a glove maker, butcher and wool dealer. He was an upstanding citizen of Stratford and held in sufficiently high esteem to be elected to the municipal office of this new small community. While he was once fined for maintaining a dung heap on the street where he lived with his family, the public records show that he paid the fine, indicating that he may as well have been a farmer.

In contrast to his father, we know little of young William's early life, except that he was the third of his parent's children, probably went to a local grammar school and probably would have gone much further than that if it had not been for the unfortunate circumstance that his father fared not too well and gradually lost his property and was then disqualified from holding any official position. So it was that young William was obliged to be an assistant to his father after the latter had returned to his trade as a butcher. While busily cutting the throats of his father's hogs, he indulged in the delight of entertaining customers, declaiming poetry and making high-spirited speeches instead of doing much work. Alas, as he was 'gainfully' employed, went on at the time, with his life experience, and then pregnant Anne, of some twenty-six years of age, took her Will in holy matrimony in the autumn of 1582. It did arouse a bit of small talk around the neighbourhood, but such gossip troubled our young Bard not in the least. However, when the baby was born 'before its due date' as proof is in the pudding, so to speak, the good Christian people of Stratford concocted a nice little scandal. This was a latter-day slap in the face by his community and a slur on his good name and that of his wife as far as he was concerned. So he packed his little family off to the city where familiarity did not breed contempt.

The widely spread reputation of our lively young man, W. Shakespeare, was considered by all and sundry as a man of education but out of his rural class and a 'rebel' by the local establishment. He decided to move to the city to escape the bondage and small-mindedness of his native home. He seemed to disappear from view for the next eight years, occasionally appearing as an apothecary, a dyer, a soldier of fortune, a public scribe and sometimes a printer, only to disappear and reappear

again in a different guise. After a time his name began to pop up with more regularity as one of those who worked for the stage. This was at a time when authors were considered persons of some importance. In this, I am not alluding to the fact that he had any instance of success, far from it. In a small way, he was initially a bit of a hack writer. Still, in a more acceptable time and with a marketing opportunity to sell works, he would possibly be claimed today, even more heroically, as one of the one per cent of playwrights, poets and film script writers who make a living from their art form. Shakespeare lived long before an author's comings and goings were worthy of the public's constant observation. Despite years of research and studies by scholars of renown to this present day, we are still much in the dark about the data of his professional career. Such are the eons of age that the world brings upon us as we mature. We are remembered for gratuitous deeds and equally soon forgotten.

Aww! But now, for the poem " The Seven Ages of Man."

All the world's a stage,
And all the men and women are merely players. They have their exits and their entrances. And one man in his time plays many parts, his acts being seven ages.

At first, the infant,
Mewling and puking in the nurse's arms, and then the whining schoolboy, with his satchel And shining morning face, creeping like a snail unwillingly to school.

And then the lover,
Sighing like furnace, with a woeful ballad
Made to his mistress's eyebrow.

Then a soldier, Full of strange oaths,
and bearded like a pard, Jealous in honour,
sudden and quick to quarrel, Seeking the bubble reputation,
Even in the cannon's mouth

And then the justice, in the fair round belly with good capon lined, With eyes severe and beard of formal cut,
Full of wise saws and modern instances, plays his part.

The sixth age shifts... into the lean and slipper-pantaloon, with spectacles on nose and pouch on side; his youthful hose, well saved, a world too wide for his shrunk shank; and his big manly voice, Turning again toward childish treble, pipes And whistles in his sound.

The last scene of all that ends this strange eventful history is second childishness and mere oblivion: without teeth, without eyes, without sound.

CHAPTER 2.

A MAN WITH A MISSION

And so we move now into the world of a scholar with a broad view of the world, humanity, and nature. Thomas Aquinas was born in 1224 in Roccasecca, near Aquino, Terra di Lavoro, Sicily [Italy] and died March 7, 1274, in Fossanova, near Terracina, Latium, Papal States; and was canonised ' Saint' on July 18, 1323. In his lifetime, he was an Italian Dominican theologian and the foremost Medieval Scholar. He developed his conclusions from the Aristotelian premise, notably in the metaphysics of personality, creation, and protective care of God or nature as a spiritual power. As a theologian, his two masterpieces, the *Summa Theologiae.*-He intended to be the sum of all known learning as explained according to the philosophy of Aristotle (384–322 BCE) and his Arabian commentators (which was being introduced to Western European thought at the time) and the theological dicta of the church. and the Summa contra gentiles a poet, who wrote some of the most gravely beautiful eucharistic hymns in the church's liturgy. His doctrinal system and the explanations and developments made by his followers are known as Thomism. (the theology of Thomas Aquinas) Although many modern Roman Catholic theologians do not find St. Thomas altogether congenial, the Roman Catholic Church recognises him as its foremost Western philosopher and theologian.

Thomas was born to parents with modest feudal land tenure, a boundary constantly disputed by the emperor and the Pope. His father was of Germanic origin; his mother hailed from later invading Norman heritage. His people were distinguished in the service of Emperor Frederick 11 during the civil strife in southern Italy between the papal and imperial forces. Thomas was placed in the monastery of Monte Cassino near his home as an oblate (i.e., offered as a prospective monk) when he was still a young boy; his family doubtless hoped that he would someday become abbot to their advantage. In 1239, after nine years in this sanctuary of spiritual and cultural life, young Thomas was forced to return to his family when the emperor expelled the monks because they were too obedient to the pope. He was then sent to the University of Naples, recently founded by the emperor, where he first encountered the scientific and philosophical works that were being translated from Greek to Arabic.

In this setting, Thomas decided to join the Friars Preachers, or Dominicans, a new religious order founded 30 years earlier, which departed from the traditional paternalistic form of government for monks to the more democratic form of the mendicant friars (i.e., religious orders whose corporate as well as personal poverty made it necessary for them to beg alms) and from the monastic life of prayer and manual labour to a more active life of preaching and teaching. By this move, he took a liberating step beyond the feudal world into which he was born and the monastic spirituality in which he was reared. A dramatic episode marked the full significance of his decision. His parents had him abducted on the road to Paris, where his wise superiors had immediately assigned him so that he would be out of the reach of his family but also so that he could pursue his studies in the most prestigious and turbulent university of the time. Thomas stubbornly opposed his family despite a year of captivity. He was finally liberated and, in the autumn of 1245, went to Paris to the convent of Saint-Jacques, the great university centre of the Dominicans; there, he studied under St. Albertus Magnus, a tremendous scholar with a wide range of intellectual interests.

Thomas spent three years in Paris, studying philosophy, and then was sent to Cologne in 1248 under the supervision of 'Albert the Great.' Albert Magnus, the older Dominican, proved to be the ideal mentor. Albert was, at the time, the leading figure in the newly prominent program of melding Christian theology with Greek and Arabic philosophy. He possessed a comprehensive grasp of the sciences of the day, which had been expanding at a dizzying pace thanks to the new availability of the Aristotelian corpus in Latin translation. Magnus' firm conviction, which became Aquinas's own, was that the Christian faith could only benefit from a profound engagement with philosophy and science.

Escape from the feudal world, rapid commitment to the University of Paris, and religious vocation to one of the new mendicant orders all meant a great deal in a world in which faith in the traditional institutional and conceptual structure was being attacked. The encounter between the gospel and the culture of his time formed the nerve centre of Thomas's position and directed its development. Usually, his work is presented as the integration into Christian thought of the recently discovered Aristotelian philosophy, in competition with the integration of Platonic thoughts effected by the Fathers of the Church during the first 12 centuries of the Christian Era. This view is correct; more radically, it should also be asserted that Thomas's work accomplished an evangelical awakening to the need for cultural and spiritual renewal in the lives of individual men and throughout the church. Thomas must be understood in his context as a mendicant religious, influenced by the evangelism of St Francis of Assisi, founder of the Franciscan order, and by the devotion to scholarship of St. Dominic, founder of the Dominican order.

When Thomas Aquinas arrived at the University of Paris, the influx of Arabian-Aristotelian science aroused a sharp reaction among believers. Several times, the church authorities tried to block the naturalism and rationalism emanating from this philosophy and, according to many ecclesiastics, seducing the younger generations. Thomas did not fear these new ideas, but, like his master Albert Magnus (and Roger Bacon, also lecturing in Paris), he studied the works of Aristotle and eventually lectured publicly on them.

For the first time in history, Christian believers and theologians were confronted with the rigorous demands of scientific rationalism. At the same time, technical progress required men to move from the rudimentary economy of an agrarian society to an urban society with production organised in trade guilds, a market economy, and a profound feeling of community. New generations of men and women, including clerics, were reacting against the traditional notion of contempt for the world and were striving for mastery over the forces of nature through their reason. The structure of Aristotle's philosophy emphasised the importance of the intelligence. Technology became a means of access to truth; mechanical arts were powers for humanising the cosmos. Thus, the dispute over the reality of universals—i.e., the question about the relation between general words such as "red" and particulars such as "this red object"—which had dominated early Scholastic philosophy, was left behind, and a coherent metaphysics of knowledge and the world was being developed.

During the summer of 1248, Aquinas left Paris with Albert, who was to assume the direction of the new faculty established by the Dominicans at the convent in Cologne. He remained there until 1252 when he returned to Paris to prepare for the degree of Master of Theology. Thomas flourished under Albert's influence, for when Albert was asked in 1252 to nominate a student to pursue an advanced degree in theology at the University of Paris, he chose Thomas, even though he was still two years younger than the minimum required age.

After taking his bachelor's degree, he received the "license to teach" at the beginning of 1256. Shortly afterwards Thomas finished the training necessary for the title and privileges of master. Thus, in 1256, he began teaching theology in one of the two Dominican schools incorporated in the University of Paris. After four years as a bachelor of theology, lecturing on the Bible and Peter Lombard's *Sentences*, Aquinas received his doctorate and was immediately appointed master of theology, once again at an earlier age than the statutes officially allowed. From 1256 until 1259, he held the Dominican chair of theology in Paris, preaching, lecturing on the Bible, and presiding over various philosophical and theological disputations.

Although some masters at the University of Paris spent decades teaching there, it was the custom of the Dominican order (as with the Franciscans) to rotate scholars through these positions. Accordingly, in 1259, Aquinas was sent back to Italy, where he spent most of the following decade in several Dominican houses of study, first in Orvieto (in Umbria) and then in Rome. During these years, while he continued to preach, lecture on the Bible, and conduct academic disputations, he found the time to develop his two most important works, the *Summa contra gentiles,* a theological synthesis that explains and defends the existence and nature of God without invoking the art in that it explores the nature of God, ethics, and human reason of the Bible; whilst his *Summa Theologiae* thesis examines the nature of God, ethics, and human reason from a practical worldly sense.

So it was that in 1268, Aquinas was asked to return to Paris for an unusual second term as master of theology. Here, he put his now venerable reputation to work in attempting to steer the philosophical conversation away from various extreme positions dividing scholars. He wrote a brief treatise arguing for a middle ground on the vexed question of whether the world could be proved to be eternal or created in time and a somewhat more extended treatise against the view that all human beings share a single intellect. These years were dominated, though, by his efforts to complete the *Summa Theologiae* and at the same time he wrote commentaries on all of Aristotle's principal works. When his second four-year term in Paris ended, he returned to Italy, this time to Naples, in 1272. During these final years, he nearly, but not quite finished both the *Summa Theologiae* and his commentary series. Instead, after a year and a half in Naples, he stopped writing, famously explaining that "All that I have written seems to me like straw compared with what has now been revealed to me." A few months later, he died in the Cistercian abbey of Fossanova on March 7, 1274. While embracing the teaching of Aristotelian science and natural law, Thomas Aquinas's radical theology was infused with his mix of Church and State laws when he wrote of the broader church. It would have been read as radical thinking in his day.

Still, he never the less applied the thinking to charitable works when he wrote the following in The Duty of Charity (Article 7, conclusions.):

" What pertains to human law can in no way detract from what pertains to natural or divine law. According to the natural order instituted by divine providence, material goods are provided to satisfy human needs. Therefore, the division and appropriation of property, which proceeds from human law, must not hinder the satisfaction of man's necessity from such goods. Equally, whatever a man has in superabundance is owed, of natural right, to the poor for their sustenance. So Ambrosius says, and it is also to be found in the Decretum Gratian (Dist. XLV11): 'The bread which you withhold belongs to the hungry; the clothing you shut away, to the naked; the money you bury in the earth is the redemption and freedom of the penniless.' But, because there are many in need, and they cannot be helped from the same source, it is left to the initiatives of the individuals to make provisions from their wealth for the assistance of those in need. If, however, there is such urgent and evident necessity that there is an immediate need for necessary sustenance, for example, a person is in the immediate danger of physical deprivation. There is no other way of satisfying his need- then he may take what is necessary from another person's goods, either openly or stealthily. Nor is this, strictly speaking, fraud or robbery."

It would be suitable even today for the leaders of Church and State and, indeed, the broader church of the brotherhood of mankind to pay heed to Aquinas's statement. For us of the first world today, be we individual or collective, are ruled by the shadiness of pride, greed, wrath, envy, lust, gluttony and sloth, which are contra to Horace's historical guidance: "to flee vice is the beginning of virtue and to have got rid of folly is the beginning of wisdom." The world of the masses of men of quiet desperation lives contrary to the seven heavenly virtues of humility, charity, chastity, gratitude, temperance, patience, and diligence, elaborated in the 13th century by St. Thomas Aquinas in his teachings.

In summarising Thomas Aquinas's thoughts on natural law and divine law, we need to remind ourselves that the great theologian thought that although humility is not the essential virtue — that honour belongs to charity (love) it is the beginning of Christian virtue because, without humility, we cannot be in a position of openness to the work of the Holy Spirit in our lives.

Aquinas's theology is embedded within the pillars of modern-day Catholic belief in the Trinity of the Almighty Father, his son Jesus, who died on the cross so that mankind could absorb the rewards of the grace of the third person of the Trinity, the Holy Spirit.

Thomas's teaching and thoughts were that although humility is not the essential virtue — that honour belongs to charity (love) — it is the beginning of Christian virtue because, without humility, we cannot be in a position of openness to the work of the Holy Spirit in our lives.

There is one other whose life and actions are worthy of consideration in this brotherhood of man's approach to living the good life in line with the golden rule of do unto others in charitable works. That man was St. Francis of Assisi.

CHAPTER 3.

FRANCIS OF ASSISI

The low-rolling Umbria hills seem to have an excellent influence upon the poetic streak of human nature, and someday I may well list the world's slender output of geniuses and tabulate according to their geographic background, for I have come to believe that highlands are the ideal breeding ground for people of poetic tendency. Little Francesco, let us call him Francis, for which he came to be known, had a natural poetic streak and was often heard singing in French but, more often than not, the native Italian tongue of the locals.

Francis was not a particularly scholarly youth although he studied Latin and French, he preferred to escape into the world of the troubadour, those lyric poets of southern France, Northern Spain and Italy. Writing in the Languedoc Provence, troubadours flourished from the late 11th to the late 13th century, Their influence was unprecedented in the history of medieval poetry. Favoured in the courts, they had a significant impact on freedom of speech, occasionally intervening in the political arena, wooing women into men's quarters with elaborate love lyrics, expanding into ballads, tales of knights of the realm, a way of conversation in matters of the heart, religion and metaphysical satire. Therefore, A troubadour invented new poems, elaborate love lyrics, stories and musical rhymes that have lasted to this day.

Francis was more fond of worldly pleasures than reading and writing; in that regard, he was no different from any youth today. He was probably expected to learn his Dad's lucrative trade as a local tailor and succeed him in the business. It may have proved so if not for a provincial war between Assisi and the neighbouring township of Perugia in 1202.

Francis had only just recovered from a severe illness when he set out with the local youth to fight. Francis already had a spiritually enlightening experience when recovering from his illness but put it aside to join in the battle. Assisi lost the battle, and Francis was imprisoned for a year. There was a big celebration of his release from prison and return to Assisi after the war had ended. Francis was urged to come to the celebrations by his companions to help him forget his recent imprisonment. Still, he slipped away into distant hills, for the old Francis Bernardone no longer existed. It is not easy to glean from his history what Francis was about. Perhaps the thought-filled statements of Thoreau on man may give a hint: "Most men lead lives of quiet desperation." I think Francis quelled his desperation by following his heart instead of his head. For the other memorable statement of Thoreau: "Every man's heart beats to the tune of a different drummer; let him follow the sound of the drummer that he hears." Francis did that, and his prayers centred around God and nature, confirming a way of life uniquely lived. Other than his mentor Jesus, who of course, it is reported died on a cross for mankind to be released from their character defects.

Francis took his place among the poorest of the poor and died in a pauper grave, body worn out long before his appointed time by a life of labour and want, his sound faith living on, as it does in all who believe solemnly in a power greater than themselves that run the show. In Francis's case, he saw it all in the natural order. He was our divine comedy of laughable wisdom, which may yet prove to be a better course of spiritual food than that of a doctorate in theology. We have not had another like him in a long time, as it would take an almost superhuman effort to accomplish or, indeed play the role of Francis in these times. Perhaps Mother Theresa of Calcutta of the 20th century did live in a Francis-conscious way. Of course, many a poet, artist and writer of note has by necessity and not choice, lived a paragraph of St. Francis's story in private poverty for the sake of their art. In the vein of social activist, Dorothy Day, Francis was not a social worker or modern-day evangelistic activist, even though he preached to more immense multitudes than any other person before or after him. He was not interested in religious doctrine or written philosophy to live by, even though he was the author of more spiritual prayers, poetic quotes and songs than almost any other.

The man later canonised as a saint was not out to form a new cult or religious school of thought. So many people followed his way of life at the time. Ultimately, his teachings and followers had no choice but to form a defined organisation in their gatherings of prayer, communal living and working tirelessly for the poor. It was not Francis' style, he was not fitted for being the head of an organisation. He had no choice but to leave such things to others of greater ambition to perform executive orders.

Francis was not diplomatic in his approach to any situation that irked him and, on more than one occasion, did what no one else had done then or since. The first impulsive act was during attendance at Easter Sunday Mass when all the local wealthy middle class displayed their finery in dress, jewellery and apparel to prove their importance. When even the priest was dressed in garments of opulent splendour and the altar itself was adorned with the finest of golden candle holders and chalices of gold, Francis jumped to his feet amid the ceremony and uttered in full voice something in the vein of any critic: No! No! No! this is not the way of God; it should not be the way of the church." It wasn't exactly those words but something similar enough to embarrass his Father and Mother seated there in their finery. Francis abruptly left the proceedings, returned to his father's business, took some of the best materials off the shelves, gathered his horse from the stable, and headed out to the nearest township. Therein, he sold all the material and his horse and went to give it all to the local Dominican friar, who refused his offer.

Francis, insulted by the priest's refusal to accept his gift, threw the loot out into the street to be gathered by passing rich and poor alike. On return home his angered Father had him locked away for a time and then hauled him before a local magistrate to admit his sorrow and repay his dues for the goods taken. In truth, Francis, in his mind, probably only took what he considered his share for fair labour to the business. He refused to yield before the Magistrate, so his father took him to the Bishop, but Francis refused to acknowledge his authority. Then and there, he stripped himself naked in the presence of Bishop and Father, announcing: "Until now I considered you Father on earth, but no more shall that be. I have but one Father now, and He is my heavenly one. Only for him will I pay homage and work for until my dying day."

On another occasion, Francis set himself as a newly appointed brother of Christ, dressed in sackcloth with a rope cord to hold his now poor man's tunic in place, and went to Rome to inform the Pope of his intention in naturally following Christ, living as a poor man, feeding the poor with bread for their stomach and spiritual harmony for their soul and encouraging others to join him in a similar lifestyle. It was to everyone's great surprise, that Francis baptised the Pope on the spot into the Christian faith of a new brotherhood. Imagine anyone doing that to a Muslim leader of our times or indeed to Adolf Hitler at the height of his program of Jewish annihilation, recommending that he embrace Jewish doctrine. Nor is it convincing Vladimir Putin to turn from Orthodox Christian to Roman Catholic! For that matter, blessing an instrument of death and forgiving it for the torture it may cause. Francis, in his latter days, did this on many an occasion.

Indeed, he had not found a cult nor a way of forced dogma. God forbid there are so many of those fanatics in our day. Nor did he promise to cure the world of viruses by some kind of spiritual means. Francis would have dispensed with them all like Mohammad marching on Mecca to voice without bloodshed a new way of belief. Francis, the inspirer of the meek, was an expert psychologist, for he understood his fellow man, he knew how to dig deep into the soul and ignite a light that in most men had all but been extinguished.

A case in point at the time was Clare, the eldest daughter of the Count of Sasso Rosso. At 18 years of age, Clare heard Francis preach during a Lenten service in the church of San Giorgio and asked him to help her live according to the gospel. On Palm Sunday in 1212, Clare secretly left her home and went to the chapel of the Portziuncu; to meet with Francis. She cut off her
long blond hair and was given a plain robe and veil in exchange for her rich gown.

Whilst Clare's family were very disappointed with her choice of vocation and tried to force her home, she refused. When her sister Catalina who took the name Agnus, joined the vocation, her family also stopped her and even beat her, but like he sister Agnus was determined to follow in her sister's vocation. Other women joined Clare and Agnus and they became known as the " Poor Ladies of San Damiano," and later " The Poor Clares". They wore no shoes, ate no meat and kept silent most of the time in a kind of permanent retreat. Clare punished her body with mortification and penance and was known to have worn a hair shirt made of pig skin for 29 years! The "Sister of St. Clare" to this very day feeds the poor and follows in similar personal sacrifice as followers of Christ and the dictates exemplified by Francis of Assisi and the Franciscan Order.

Francis was a typical representative of a saintly medieval mentality, with an unusual acceptance of disease and other afflictions including poor hygiene that to his mind could be eradicated with a bar of soap and a cup of soup. Francis himself ate moulding bread from the bins of Assisi whilst feeding the poor of the city on the best of dough given as charity by kindly folk. Who can foresee but a man who visualised Assisi upside down, the poor being on the top and the rich on the bottom? He spent his nights in prayer, fasting into hallucinations, suffering stigmata on both hands and feet. This was after his visit to Mount Alverno, where he may well have penetrated his wrist and feet in an imitation of Christ during a trance-like state, not realising in reality what he had done.

To examine further serves no purpose, but followers at the time saw it as a miracle. They are the simple people of this world who are devoid of inner complications. Those perform simple tasks with an honest, sober willingness to serve. They, too, gain the respect and possible affection of the masses because they excel in stewardship, which they rightfully see as their duty.

Then there are those like St. Francis, who seem so simple because they are so hopelessly complicated, and that is, at best, the only hope we have of explaining them. They are the ones who are most likely to move the world out of its humdrum everyday existence and do so with far more infinitely far-reaching beneficial results than the greatest of conquering heroes. Then there are the masses of men who muddle their way through life, devoid of its meaning and spiritual significance.

It is in our soul search to emulate Francis of Assisi but do we need more will to follow such a righteous path of self-sacrifice? As a finale to this chapter, it is worth considering St. Francis's prayer in that regard.

Lord, make me an instrument of your peace;
where there is hatred, let me sow love;
where there is injury, pardon;
where there is doubt, faith;
where there is despair, hope;
where there is darkness, light;
and where there is sadness, bring joy.

O Divine Master,
grant that I may not so much seek to be consoled as to console;
to be understood, as to understand;
to be loved, as to love;
for it is in giving that we receive,
it is in pardoning that we are pardoned,
and it is in dying that we are born to Eternal Life.

Amen.

CHAPTER 4

MOTHER TERESA OF CALCUTTA

"By blood, I am Albanian. By citizenship, an Indian. By faith, I am a Catholic nun. As to my calling, I belong to the world. As to my heart, I belong entirely to the Heart of Jesus." Small in stature, and rocklike in faith, Mother Teresa of Calcutta was entrusted with the mission of proclaiming GodÂ's thirsting love for humanity, especially for the poorest of the poor. *"God still loves the world and He sends you and me to be His love and His compassion to the poor."* She was a soul filled with the light of Christ, on fire with love for Him and burning with one desire: *"to quench His thirst for love and souls."*

This luminous messenger of God's love was born on 26 August 1910 in Skopje, a city situated at the crossroads of Balkan history. The youngest of the children born to Nikola and Drane Bojaxhiu, she was baptised Gonxha Agnes, received her First Communion at the age of five and a half and was confirmed in November 1916. From the day of her First Holy Communion, a love for souls was within her. Her father's sudden death when Gonxha was about eight years old left the family in financial straits. Drane raised her children firmly and lovingly, greatly influencing her daughter's character and vocation. Gonxha's religious formation was further assisted by the vibrant Jesuit parish of the Sacred Heart in which she was much involved.

At the age of eighteen, moved by a desire to become a missionary, Gonxha left her home in September 1928 to join the Institute of the Blessed Virgin Mary, known as the Sisters of Loretto, in Ireland. There she received the name Sister Mary on 10 September 1946 during the train ride from Calcutta to

Darjeeling for her annual retreat, Mother Teresa received her *"inspiration,"* her *"call within a call."* On that day, in a way she would never explain, Jesus's thirst for love and souls took hold of her heart and the desire to satiate His thirst became the driving force of her life. Over the course of the next weeks and months, using interior locutions and visions, Jesus revealed to her the desire of His heart for *"victims of love"* who would *"radiate His love on souls."* Come be My light," He begged her. *"I cannot go alone."* He revealed His pain at the neglect of the poor, His sorrow at their ignorance of Him and His longing for their love. He asked Mother Teresa to establish a religious community, Missionaries of Charity, dedicated to the service of the poorest of the poor. Nearly two years of testing and discernment passed before Mother Teresa received permission to begin. On August 17, 1948, she dressed for the first time in a white, blue-bordered sari and passed through the gates of her beloved Loretto convent to enter the world of the poor.

After a short course with the Medical Mission Sisters in Patna, Mother Teresa returned to Calcutta and found temporary lodging with the Little Sisters of the Poor. On 21 December she went for the first time to the slums. She visited families, washed the sores of some children, cared for an old man lying sick on the road and nursed a woman dying of hunger and TB. She started each day in communion with Jesus in the Eucharist and then went out, rosary in her hand, to find and serve Him in *"the unwanted, the unloved, the uncared for."* After some months, she was joined, one by one, by her former students.

On 7 October 1950, the new congregation of the Missionaries of Charity was officially established in the Archdiocese of Calcutta. By the early 1960s, Mother Teresa began to send her Sisters to other parts of India. The Decree of Praise granted to the Congregation by Pope Paul VI in February 1965 encouraged her to open a house in Venezuela. It was soon followed by foundations in Rome and Tanzania and, eventually, on every continent. Starting in 1980 and continuing through the 1990s, Mother Teresa opened houses in almost all of the communist countries, including the former Soviet Union, Albania and Cuba.

To respond better to both the physical and spiritual needs of the poor, Mother Teresa founded the *Missionaries of Charity Brothers* in 1963, in 1976 the *contemplative branch* of the Sisters, in 1979 the *Contemplative Brothers*, and in 1984 the *Missionaries of Charity Fathers.* Yet her inspiration was not limited to those with religious vocations. She formed the *Co-Workers of Mother Teresa* and the *Sick and Suffering Co-Workers,* people of many faiths and nationalities with whom she shared her spirit of prayer, simplicity, sacrifice and her apostolate of humble works of love. This spirit later inspired the *Lay Missionaries of Charity*. In answer to the requests of many priests, in 1981 Mother Teresa also began the *Corpus Christi Movement for Priests* as a *"little way of holiness"* for those who desire to share in her charism and spirit.

During the years of rapid growth, the world began to turn its eyes towards Mother Teresa and the work she had started. Numerous awards, beginning with the Indian Padmashri Award in 1962 and notably the Nobel Peace Prize in 1979, honoured her work, while an increasingly interested media began to follow her activities. She received both prizes and attention *"for the glory of God and in the name of the Lord and the poor."*

The whole of Mother Teresa's life and labour bore witness to the joy of loving, the greatness and dignity of every human person, the value of little things done faithfully and with love, and the surpassing worth of friendship with God. But there was another heroic side of this great woman that was revealed only after her death. Hidden from all eyes, hidden even from those closest to her, was her interior life marked by an experience of a deep, painful and abiding feeling of being separated from God, even rejected by Him, along with an ever-increasing longing for His love. She called her inner experience, *"the darkness."* The "painful night" of her soul, which began around the time she started her work for the poor and continued to the end of her life, led Mother Teresa to an ever more profound union with God. Through the darkness, she mystically participated in the thirst of Jesus, in God's painful and burning longing for love, and she shared in the interior desolation of the poor.

During the last years of her life, despite increasingly severe health problems, Mother Teresa continued to govern her Society and respond to the needs of the poor and the Church. By 1997, Mother Teresa's Sisters numbered nearly 4,000 members and were established in 610 foundations in 123 countries of the world. In March 1997 she blessed her newly-elected successor as Superior General of the Missionaries of Charity and then made one more trip abroad. After meeting Pope John Paul II for the last time, she returned to Calcutta and spent her final weeks receiving visitors and instructing her Sisters. On 5 September Mother Teresa's earthly life came to an end. She was given the honour of a state funeral by the Government of India and her body was buried in the Mother House of the Missionaries of Charity. Her tomb quickly became a place of pilgrimage and prayer for people of all faiths, rich and poor alike. Mother Teresa left a testament of unshakable faith, invincible hope and extraordinary charity. Her response to Jesus' plea, "Come be My light," made her a Missionary of Charity, "Mother to the poor," a symbol of compassion to the world, and a living witness to the thirsting love of God.

Where did Mother Teresa find the strength and the ability to continue to serve in such a life-giving way for so many years? How did she develop her heart and love for the poor? And where did her strength of character and passion ion sion to serve come from?

The answers are found in her daily actions, particularly in her regular devotion to prayer and entering into the presence of God through faith practices, most remarkably in silence.

Mother Teresa fostered a deeply intimate relationship with Jesus throughout her life. Her practice of silence created room for prayer and space for her relationship with God to grow.

For Mother Teresa silence was a prerequisite to prayer and the ability to meet with God. Prayer, through the means of silence, took upon itself to form a deep intimacy with God and with Jesus. " And when the time comes and we can't pray it is n very simple: If Jesus is in my heart let Him pray, let me allow Him to pray in me, to talk to his father in the silence of my heart, she would say. " If I cannot speak, He will speak: If I cannot pray, He will pray."

Mother Teresa had a devotion to the Virgin Mary too: " To thee I come, before thee I stand, sinful and sorrowful. O Mother of the Word incarnate, despise not my petitions, but in thy mercy hear and answer me. Amen."

Less than two years after her death, given Mother Teresa's widespread reputation of holiness and the favours being reported, Pope John Paul II permitted the opening of her Cause of Canonization. On 20 December 2002, he approved the decrees of her heroic virtues and miracles.

CHAPTER 5.

A MESSAGE OF LEADERSHIP

General Sir John Monash was indeed an excellent Australian. Arguably our greatest military commander – I would certainly argue it. An accomplished engineer, a talented musician and eventually a highly successful businessman. He was complex and passionate. He had his personal flaws and relationship difficulties, as we all do. He was proudly Jewish in an age and nation where it was not to one's advantage to be so. Despite this, his intellect, his ambition, his innovation and his astonishing competence allowed him to rise above prejudice and racism and enrich our nation to this very day with contributions that we still come here to honour. According to the author Colin McInnes Monash's presence and prestige 'made anti-Semitism, as a "respectable" attitude, impossible in Australia'. God knows our modern society would do better to follow suit and judge the man rather than impose the stereotype – but then few men of Monash's qualities can convince humanity to put aside prejudice.

John Monash was born in Melbourne in 1865 and educated at Scotch College, then the University of Melbourne – his university education was not a smooth passage. While he hugely valued scholarship he was equally enamoured of the more social aspects of a young university student's life. He was also distracted by the necessity of earning money to support his education and family. Notably, he started as an Arts student with bachelor's degrees in engineering and law. At an early stage, he began applying his academic knowledge to improve his business and military outcomes. He brought his engineering and mathematical skills into the science of gunnery by designing and constructing an artillery training the gun that revolutionised how the coastal artillery trained. He wrote a treatise called Hundred Tips for Company Commanders, which became required reading for all those who followed.

From early on in his career, he had an excellent rapport with people – up, down and across. Most were captured by his passion and commitment. His effect on people was well described by the chief technical advisor Hyman Herman in the State Electricity Commission, who stated; 'he was a great leader and a genius in getting to the heart of any problem and finding its solution ... the ablest, biggest-minded and biggest-hearted man I have ever known'. Those who got to know and understand him remained supporters for life.

By 1914, he had, in civilian life, established himself as a pillar of Melbourne society, lecturing and examining engineering at university. Involved in a wide range of community activities, including the Boy Scouts, and several prominent appointments such as the graduates association's chairman, the university club president, and the Victorian Institute of Engineers.

With the outbreak of war, Monash started slowly, taking on roles in intelligence and then briefly as a chief censor. Eventually, his worth shone through, and he was appointed commander of the 4th infantry brigade and then promoted to brigadier. His brigade trained in Egypt and landed at Gallipoli on the morning of the 26th of April 1915. The brigade was involved in many significant actions and suffered heavy casualties before it was pulled back to Egypt in early December.

Around this time and throughout the remainder of his military career, Monash was continuously subjected to whispering campaigns launched by those less than fond of him. These ranged from false accusations that he was born and educated in Germany to claims he spoke poor English, all the way to rumours that he had been shot as a spy. Despite these retrograde efforts by detractors, Monash was promoted to Major General in July 1916 and placed in command of the 3rd Australian division. The division was involved in months of severe fighting and trench warfare in France from November 1916 until they progressed to full-scale operations from June 1917 onward.

In June 1918, he was promoted to Lieutenant General and appointed the Australian Army Corps commander. During this period, he planned and directed a series of determined and effective actions commencing in July 1918 with the masterful and meticulously planned breach of the German line at the battle of Hamel. Eight thousand (8,000) synchronised troops supported by artillery, tanks and aircraft attacked Hamel at dawn on 4 July 1918. One thousand (1,000) of these were American soldiers, the first to be commanded in combat by another nation much to the displeasure of US Commander Pershing at the time. The battle had been planned to take 90 minutes. It was over in 93 with all objectives taken and over 1,500 German soldiers taken prisoner. The battle for Amiens came next - described by Ludendorff as the black day for the German army. Then came the penetration of the Hindenburg line by 5th October 1918, and the Germans sued for peace.

His successes in the war could be attributed, among many things, to his pre-war study of all the primary 'new' weaponry that emerged at that time, including the tank and the aeroplane, artillery, machine guns, and decoy targets. He was a great believer in employing modern communications, including the radio and in achieving situational awareness through aerial reconnaissance. While others had mastered employing individual capabilities, no one else synchronised the effects of all the capabilities together like Monash. He maintained that:

The proper role of infantry was not to expend itself upon heroic physical effort, not to wither away under merciless machine-gun fire, not to impale itself on hostile bayonets, but on the contrary, to advance under the maximum possible protection of the maximum possible array of mechanical resources, in the form of guns, machine-guns, tanks, mortars and aeroplanes; to advance with as little impediment as possible; to be relieved as far as possible of the obligation to fight their way forward.

Monash approached battles as he approached engineering projects in his civilian employment---by coordinating all the key elements in great detail. He encouraged a working environment in which innovation was expected and input demanded. Monash promoted professional debate and gave commanders freedom of action. Under his leadership, for the first time, all fighting elements and supporting services had a solid comprehension of each other's operational methods and goals. They knew what they were doing and why they were doing it.

PM Lloyd George, Winston Churchill, and (later) Field Marshall Montgomery maintained that Monash was the outstanding general on the Western Front because of his 'creative originality."

As a military commander, he was a man whose natural feeling was to serve first. He was deeply concerned and committed to the welfare and, quite starkly compared to some of his peers and superiors, to the survival of the men under his command. Keenly conscious of not only the carnage of the Western Front but of the crippling impact of battlefield losses on Australian society, he acted with a sort of "ruthless compassion" when planning attacks. He sought to completely overwhelm the enemy through precise organisation and detailed preparation, ensuring that every advantage was offered to his force with nothing left to chance.

He institutionalised what we now routinely call joint and combined arms warfare, and to this very day, the Army's significant annual combined arms training activity is named Exercise Hamel.

After the armistice, the war was far from over for John Monash. He was entrusted with the task of demobilising and repatriating the 180 thousand surviving Australian troops so that they might return to society as useful citizens after experiencing the horrors of war. He arranged for them to undergo training in the United Kingdom while the massive task of planning and executing demobilisation and transportation continued. He oversaw the convalescence and rehabilitation of those who had been wounded and arranged for the return of the wives and children of those who had met and married war brides in the United Kingdom or France. He involved himself in the welfare of his men, understanding that having asked them to give him their all in combat, he was ever obligated to care for them when they had done so.

Upon returning from the war, Monash's energy enabled him to continue with his prominent community involvement and contribution to some organisations. Some of his appointments included royal commissioner to investigate the police strike of 1923, head of the Victorian State Electrical Commission, membership of the Commonwealth Defence Council and the Walter and Eliza Hall Institute, service as a Rhodes scholarship selector, President of the Australian Association for the Advancement of Science, and Honorary Vice-chancellor of the University of Melbourne.

He worked tirelessly for many community organisations and significantly influenced the life and affairs of his alma mater, Melbourne University. He became a famous and revered figure on many ex-service occasions. Notably, he also contributed to establishing the ANZAC Day ceremonies and the design choice for the Shrine of Remembrance. His achievements were legion, and his influence remarkable.

Monash's example teaches us the value of diversity of culture, viewpoint, and approach. It teaches us the value of a sound education, academic discipline, and applied knowledge to generate innovation. It teaches us to care for our people and our community before ourselves. In a speech to students at Melbourne University, he gave some advice that still resonates today. He told them: "Make it your creed to equip yourself for life, not solely for your benefit but for the whole community." This simple, selfless philosophy gave rise to one of our most outstanding citizens.

All of us who aspire to any form of leadership can have no better example than General Sir John Monash. His speech was made at the Beefsteak Club in 1926 to an influential gathering of Melbourne businessmen on the success of good leadership in war is worthy of repeating here:

"War does not lend itself greatly to philosophic thoughts; it rests more upon considerations of expediency than principles. The application of principles, even where possible, is generally subconscious. Time and circumstances rarely permit ordered reasoning or deliberately formed judgements. The successful exercise of leadership must, therefore, in the end, rest upon the degree of success with which man can make his decisions and make them soundly, without that detailed review of the relevant data, and that process of deliberate reasoning which is the customary mental process applied to most other human affairs.

The capacity to form judgements rapidly and soundly is more temperamental than intellectual. A well-stored mind, a well-exercise mentality, and a fund of varied experiences in the affairs of life are necessary stock-in-trade. But these would avail a man's little war if he had not the right temperament for that environment."

"A successful leader must be unemotional to the extent of being callous to the external influences that evoke loy or sorrow, elation or despondency; he must be indifferent to praise or blame. He must persevere calmly and dispassionately with the business at hand, undisturbed either by the menace of imminent calamity or the exultation of success. He must be patient to a degree. He must have determination and steadfastness of purpose of a very high order. He must have an exalted confidence in himself and the correctness of his judgement, amounting to an intellectual arrogance. His capacity to appreciate the working of the minds of others must be automatic and swift. His personality must be of a kind that inspires confidence in others and which demonstrates their instinct to exercise independent judgment."

It may be thought but it is generally considered that personal popularity among the troops is essential to successful leadership. This is so far from the truth that the contrary proposition can be argued. A successful leader must be unemotional to the extent of being callous...The popularity of a war leader is, in the last resort, gaged by the rank and file, not from his contact with them and their impressions of his personality, but by the success of his organisation and command. A force that finds itself well-equipped, well fed and well quartered, which can achieve victories in battle without severe losses, well speedily elevate its leaders in its regard and esteem even if it has rare personal contact with them."

"He should be, in short, temperamentally, a paragon of excellence, which, I fear, none of us, despite earnest aspirations, ever ultimately reach."

"The highest and most crucial task of a leader is creating and maintaining the morale of his men. The practical test of this is their collective readiness to allow themselves to be used as instruments in his hands for the execution of his plans. The larger the military formation, the more complex the task because the leader is increasingly removed from personal contact with the rank and file and must, therefore, rely more and more on the cooperation of intermediate commanders and staff. Hence, the measure of success rests upon the power of inspiration."

"A commander of whatever grade holds his subordinates in the hollow of his hand. He has the power to make or break men at his whim and pleasure. This power is rarely curbed, even if it may sometimes be exercised unjustly and wantonly. It is more expected that the authority of the commander in his treatment of subordinates should be upheld under all circumstances than that occasional wrongs and petty tyrannies should be addressed, And that is why it happened but rarely and only in aggravated and sustained cases that acts of arbitrary and unjust treatment of subordinates were even visited upon by a senior commander." This extract from Sir John Monash's speech emphasises the importance of understanding the need for leadership in most situations in our world and the qualities of leadership for reference purposes in dealing with the masses in war and peace.

Monash displayed great military skills, a powerful intellect and inspiring leadership qualities. He impressed his soldiers and higher command. In June 1918 he was promoted to lieutenant-general and appointed to command the Australian Corps. British leaders of the time, such as Prime Minister David Lloyd George confirmed Monash was among the first under fire at Gallipoli and the only Australian brigade commander among the original troops not killed or evacuated as wounded. By 1918, he was in charge of the entire Australian Corps. In this same year, King George V knighted him on the battlefield for Monash's leadership of 208,000 men under his command, including 50,000 inexperienced Americans. Monash planned the attack on the German defences in the Battle of the Hindenburg Line between 16 September and 5 October 1918. The Allies eventually breached the Hindenburg Line by 5 October, and the war was essentially over. in the Battle of Hamel.

Monash University is widely recognized as one of Australia's leading universities and is highly respected both domestically and internationally. It consistently ranks among the top universities globally and is known for its excellence in teaching and research across the world in various disciplines.

Famous quotes of John Monash:

"Equip yourself for life, not solely for your benefit, but for the benefit of the whole community."

"We can learn to see each other and see ourselves in each other and recognize that human beings are more alike than we are unalike."

CHAPTER 6.

GANDHI'S WORK & SPEECHES

It surprised me somewhat, considering his lifetime diet of raw foods and simple tastes, to find that Mohandas Karamchand Gandhi was born, not of peasant stock, but of a wealthy political family in the princely state of Porbandar, Gujarat, West India. At the time of his birth in 1869, his father, Karamchand was Chief Minister for the area and had taught Gandhi from childhood political astuteness that would serve him well in life. Gandhi's lifetime pursuit of the perfect mental, physical and spiritual diet for his being was from the indoctrination of his devout mother, an adherent of the Jain religion. She taught him the tenets of her faith: the sanctity of life, vegetarianism, abstinence from alcohol, fasting for self-purification, and mutual tolerance across creeds and sects. These principles were the framework to help guide his adult political life. At the age of nineteen, he was sent to University College in London where he studied law and graduated in 1891 and trained as a barrister of the Inner Temple. He failed to find a job in India as a barrister, so he took a post in 1893 for a one-year appointment in Natal in South Africa but he remained there for the next twenty years championing the legal rights of the Indian community and there he adopted his strategy of non-cooperation.

An incident in the early 1890s one day in South Africa was revealing. As was expected in those days two Indians walking along a pavement were expected to walk in the gutter when approached by white folk. On this occasion, as they passed Gandhi reportedly remarked to his Indian companion: " It has always been a mystery to me' he stated without anger: " how men can feel themselves honoured by the humiliation of their fellow beings." He was twenty-two at the time and such audacity in the face of any white South African was a sign of things to come when he would shake the world with his advocacy and belief in 'Satyagraha,' the name he later gave to non-violent resistance to British rule in India.

Gandhi returned to India in 1914, at the beginning of World War 1. He joined the Indian National Congress, campaigning for civil rights and Indian self-government. It was in that first year that he initiated protests against social injustice, which continued for the rest of his life. Soon appointed leader of the Congress, he introduced non-violent boycotts of British Institutions. He was tried for sedition and imprisoned until 1924. On release, he withdrew from politics to travel around India for the next three years promoting his crafts and the plight of the 'Untouchables' (Dalits), the lowest rank of India's caste system. He married and continued on his passive-aggressive campaign cumulating in his 1930's 'Salt March.,' where he called thousands of followers to march to the ocean to make salt, to campaign against the tax on salt that the British had imposed on India. To those followers who feared being jailed by the British for this unlawful march, he simply stated: "There are only 40,000 British in India and we are over 400,000,000. They can't jail us all."

He did ultimately land himself back in jail but not over the " Salt March.' It was his resolve not to support British India's wartime role when he launched in 1939 a "Quit India" Campaign against British domination. He was jailed in 1942 with other Congress leaders after negotiations for Independence failed. When Independence finally came, he was opposed to the Mountbatten plan of dividing the country on religious grounds, thus forming two states, one of India and the other of Pakistan. This of course suited British political influences after World War, as they sought to checkmate Stalin's Russia from taking over oil-rich areas surrounding India and Pakistan which the West ultimately controlled. Gandhi's lifestyle and beliefs ultimately were the cause of his assassination by an extremist Hindu in 1948.

"To achieve anything of notability in life you not only have to have persistence, you need to be stubborn." He paused for a brief moment, adjusting his glasses and continued: " In my lifetime, I spoke of many things, I always had an inner voice guiding me. The spiritual force emphasised truth, non-violence, love, compassion and selfless concern for the wellbeing of others. It was the way I chose to live, the way of action by example." I quickly piped up: " But what about the violence caused to you and others in your promotion of non-violence in all things?" Gandhi replied: " From my youth and my Mother's Jainism religion I took the principles of not harm and developed the principle of ' truth force' on life. I hoped to win the people over by changing their hearts and minds and advocating non-violence in all things. I read many books on religions, but I always remained a committed Hindu as I saw so much hypocrisy in organised religions."

What spiritual leadership did Gandhi gain the most from? Gandhi When asked that question Gandhi replied: "Jesus' Sermon on the Mount and Leo Tolstoy." "Huh, Tolstoy, on the same spiritual plain as Jesus?" Grandi had responded. "it was the philosophies he wrote relating to his time, and I with my spiritual voice as a guide, adapted and applied those by way of example to myself as much as to others." The enquirer had pressed him for more: "Pray tell." He asked. "Well," Gandhi said: "in the words of Tolstoy, everyone thinks of changing the world, but no one thinks of changing himself.' If you look for perfection you will never be content. We can know that we know nothing, and that is the highest degree of human wisdom."

I recalled how his time in South Africa as a young man, Gandhi had been disgusted with the treatment of Indians by the white settlers there. He exhorted his countrymen to observe truthfulness in business and reminded them that their responsibility was the greatest since their conduct would be seen as a reflection of their country. He asked them to forget about religious and cast differences, to give up unsanitary habits, and to demonstrate suitability for citizenship by showing they deserved it. He spent the next twenty years there and finally gained Indian citizenship rights. On his return to India, his immediate problem was to settle his relatives and associates in an ashram- "a group life lived in a religious spirit."

I was reminded of Gandhi's Tolstoy's happiness philosophy: "A quiet secluded life in the country, with the possibility of being useful to people to whom it is easy to be good, and to who is not accustomed to having well done to them; then work which I hope may be of some use; then rest, nature, books, music, love for one's neighbour- such is my idea of happiness." Gandhi responded: "My Ashram was a small model of a whole moral and religious ideal. The community did not enforce on its inmates any theology or ritual, but only a few simple rules of personal conduct. It was more like a large fan mill than a monastery, it was filled with children and senior citizens, the uneducated and American and European scholars, devout followers and thinly disguised sceptics- a melting pot of different and sometimes opposing ideas, living peacefully and usefully with each other. I was considered the moral Father of the Ashram and would fast as penance when a wrong was committed within its walls. Everyone was bound to me only by love and a fear of hurting me. It was there I learnt to take responsibility for every method that instilled a truth force that I called 'Satyagraha.' Nowadays you would call it a force that is inherent to the truth of non-violent action."

When he failed to convince authorities of various inequalities that Indians were subject to under British rule, he went on a hunger strike as a protest which drew media attention to his cause. He was dismayed over the British refusal to grant Indian independence which resulted in a violent turn of events, copious correspondence with the Government and civil unrest during and after WW11. It was only after he inspired love in both Hindus and Muslims for him, that he was enabled to control the violence when he was threatening too fast until death to get Indian independence. It was suggested to Gandhi: "It seemed you used eating sparingly and fasting as the main means of convincing the British authorities to reduce taxes, change the status quo about class and ultimately gain independence. "I hoped to win people over to change their hearts and minds, advocating non-violence in all things, by making self-sacrifice in all bodily discipline, in food intake especially the type of food eaten which so often links with the spiritual and religious culture of the times. Occasional severe fasting to draw attention to a particular matter had the best result in effecting change "I never did get the diet thing right for myself though and tried many times what you might call today ' fad diets.' I even wrote a book on that subject."

We may draw Gandhi's attention to British law being reminded of his march to the sea to make salt and his prospects of being arrested for breaking the law. He was asked about his making salt protest: "The march to the sea with followers to protest the British Salt Tax was the most controversial act of mass civil disobedience that the world at large had awakened to, don't you agree?" He responded: " My task was done to win or perish." he added. " Then it was up to the Working Committee of Congress to show the way and then it was up to each Indian to follow the lead." He added: "No one who believes in non-violence, as creed, need, therefore, sit still. "

My compact with Congress ends as soon as I am arrested. In that case…Wherever possible, civil disobedience of salt laws should be started. These laws can be violated in three different ways; by manufacture, by possession of contraband salt, or by the carrying away of natural salt deposits on the seashores, all are likewise a violation of the law. In short, you may choose any one or all of these devices to break the salt monopoly." Gandhi had not finished making his point: "We can refuse to pay taxes if we have the requisite strength. We are not content with this alone.….other similar measures may be adopted. I stress one condition, the pledge of truth, as the only means for the attainment of home rule must be faithfully kept." he went on to say: " Much can be done in many other ways besides these. The Liquor and foreign clothing shops are picketed." Gandhi himself led by example weaving his cloth and making his clothing and he did not drink alcohol. "lawyers can give up the practice.

The public servants can resign from their posts do not despair. The number of government servants in this country does not exceed a few hundred thousand. What about the rest? A Public Service collector will not be able to afford the number of servants he has got today, he will be his servant. Our starving millions have no means to afford the enormous Public service expenditure. If, therefore, we are sensible enough, let us bid goodbye to government employment, no matter if it is the post of judge or police. Let all who are cooperative with government, in one way or another…withdraw their co-operation and support in as many ways as possible." He went on with his means of rejecting payment of taxes, withdrawing children from Government schools, etc etc." "I have faith in the righteousness of our cause and the purity of our weapons."

The civil disobedience marches and Gandhi's mobilisation of peaceful non-aggression continued for the remainder of his days, until the day of Indian Independence. It was the way the British had its say in control by way of the Mountbatten plan that disturbed Gandhi. Whilst he was pleased to see progress, be it not perfection, he took to his sleeping mat in protest whilst the Congress argued about the process of breaking up India and Pakistan into two countries. He strongly opposed the partition of India at independence in 1947 and he refused to eat for some time. In 1947 he was assassinated by a Hindu extremist, who saw him as too accommodating of India's Muslims.

Poverty in India remains a major challenge despite overall reductions in the last several decades as its economy grows. According to an IMF paper, extreme poverty, defined by the World Bank as living on US$1.9 or less in purchasing power terms, in India was as low as 0.8% in 2019, and the country managed to keep it at that level in 2020 despite the unprecedented outbreak of Covid-19. A 2020 study from the World Economic Forum found "Some 220 million Indians sustained on an expenditure level of less than 12 cents US/day—the poverty line for rural India—by the last headcount of the poor in India in 2013." Around 26 per cent of India's population lives below the poverty line, which is defined today as 14 cents per day." said officials.

"This is the other world which can be characterised as the India of the Common People, constituting more than three-fourths of the population and consisting of all those whom the growth has, by and large, bypassed,"

Gandhi by his word and deeds may be summed up in his mission for his fellowman by his following statement:

'You must be the change you wish to see in the world."

CHAPTER 7.

THE KING OF CIVIL RIGHTS

On the 5th of April 1968, the day after the assassination of Martin Luther King, United States Attorney-General Robert Kennedy delivered a speech in Cleveland Ohio. It was a short but sharp critical attack on hatred and prejudice. "What has violence accomplished? " he asked. "What has it ever created? No martyr's cause has ever been stilled by an assassin's bullet...No one, no matter where he lives or what he does, can be certain who will suffer from a senseless act of bloodshed."

"Some may think it was my Brother John's killers, others the Mafia, and still others think it was done under the Instruction of Hoover who detested my investigation into organised crime, others think the CIA in the shadows. I know, but it is best to let it go, as these men in the shadows are paying their price for their folly now."

On 16th March 1968, he declared: "I do not run for the presidency merely to oppose any man, but to propose new policies. I run because I am convinced this country is on a perilous course and because I have such strong feelings about what must be done and I feel that I am obliged to do all I can."

I recall how King came into prominence as an outspoken leader of boycotting in civil rights activism. The segregation of black Americans from whites came to a head on a bus in the township of Montgomery, Alabama, when a young black seamstress took a seat in the bus reserved only for white folk. When the driver asked Rosa Parks to move to the back she refused. The State's segregation laws resulted in her arrest which propelled African Americans to boycott Montgomery's buses. This in turn produced a historic US Supreme Court decision outlawing racial segregation on public transport. The leader in that boycott was a young Baptist Minister with a Ph. D in theology under his belt, Dr. Martin Luther King. Jr.

He was born on 15th January 1929 as Michael Luther and changed his name from Michael to Martin. He had been so impressed by the Reformation theologian Martin Luther
He had obtained his theology degree at Boston University and took up as resident minister of the local Baptist Church in Montgomery when the bus boycott took place. It spurred him on to co-found a civil rights organisation, the Southern Christian Leadership Conference in 1957. He survived a stabbing at a book launch in 1958 and moved back to Atlanta where he became a pastor in a Baptist church in his old neighbourhood in 1960. In 1963 the Christian Conference under his leadership marched on Washington for jobs and freedom. President Kennedy was initially opposed to it, as he was concerned it would retard the passage of civil rights legislation being enacted.

King eventually won the right to the March with a less stringent tone. The campaign demanded an end to racial segregation in schools, meaningful civil rights legislation including a law prohibiting racial discrimination in employment, protection of civil rights workers from brutality, a $2 minimum wage for workers and self-government for the largely black district of Columbia. The march proved a resounding success with a turnout of 250,000 people. This was his finest hour and when he delivered his " I Have a Dream" speech, electrified the crowd.
It is considered one of the finest speeches in American oratory. Using the rector's skills as a Minister and his biblical knowledge, he took the old European metaphors of the New World for whites as a promised land for the poor and oppressed and applied them to Black Americans. By 1968 he could have rested on his laurels had he desired to. He had won the hearts of the masses five years

before with his speech to that large audience, had seen the passing of the Civil Rights Act in 1964 and won the Noble Peace Prize. But in March 1968 he embarked on a new campaign to beat poverty and was in Memphis Tennessee, supporting striking African Americans when he was assassinated. Five weeks after his death, demonstrators began to show up in Washington D.C. for his so-called 'Peoples Campaign.' It had been Kings' final catch cry, without his leadership and inspirational rallying ability only 7,000 turned up- a far cry from his 1961 rally. It was to be in the economic Bill of Rights that the poor people would have full consideration but the campaign demand was never enacted.

The night before he died, 3rd April 1968, he gave a personal, poignant and eerily prophetic speech to striking garbage collectors for whom he was rallying. Reflecting on his recovery from the stab wounds he received in 1958 and his mortality: 'Longevity has its place. But I'm not concerned about that now I'm happy, tonight. I'm not worried about anything. I'm not fearing any man.' The very next day he was killed by a bullet from the assassin's gun, as he stood on the balcony of the Lorraine Motel where he had been staying.

Many murders and violent acts were committed at the height of the civil rights unrest in America's deep South in the 1950s and 1960s. Like John and Bobby Kennedy and Martin Luther King Jr. another that resonated high on the list that fired public reaction was the assassination of African American Medgar Evers. It took thirty years after the tragedy and two subsequent trials, with failed attempts to reach a verdict before police arrested Byron de la Beckwith - a former fertiliser salesman and member of the Ku Klux Klan and charged him with the murder. The body of Medgar Evers had to be exhumed for an autopsy and it was found to be surprisingly in an excellent state of preservation perhaps because of the embalming technique applied back then, or maybe it was because he was such a good man in his lifetime, that the spirits of the God of his understanding saw to it that the body remained in good order so that the culprit responsible for shooting him was found out. Following the retrial, Evers's body was reburied in a second funeral, enabling his grown-up children to say goodbye properly.

The common man it seems to me, in King's time here and my own, was caught up in the everyday circumstances of his life, providing for himself and his family, chasing wants as much as needs. The question was asked of Martin Luther King."The masses of men don't seem to have the time for just causes anymore." Dr. King responded, acutely aware of the intent of the underlying question: "Rarely do we find men willingly engaged in hard, solid thinking. There is an almost universal quest for easy answers and half-baked solutions. Nothing pains some people more than having to think." He was then asked: "So how do you change distractions of life and lack of thought to do constructive things for the benefit of not only yourself but others?"
Dr King, without hesitation, responded: " Every man must decide whether he will walk in the light of creative altruism or the darkness of destructive selfishness." The questioner persisted: "But what of the duty of mankind on an everyday level?" I asked. "He has his duty to look after his family, to work for his daily bread, to feed them, to educate his children, to pay his home mortgage and put enough aside for a rainy day."

Martin sat forward to emphasise his next point. "That is all fine if he first has well-paid employment, is not being victimised because of the colour of his skin or is segregated against so that he can't get an education or a job in the first instance." he then
 added: "There is nothing more tragic than to find an individual bogged down in the length of life, devoid of breath." another

reported questioned him further on that point: "So you think that very same man should change his priorities, put his family second for the greater good?" Martin Luther's response was intense. "An individual cannot start living until he can rise above the narrow confines of his individualistic concerns to the broader concerns of humanity." The reporter was now in the thrust of his argument: "I am not advocating that the individual should only be concerned for his circumstance but work for the greater good of all concerned, but there has to be a balance."
Dr King responded in kind. "All labour that uplifts humanity has dignity and importance and should be undertaken with painstaking excellence." "We must use time creatively, in the knowledge that time is always ripe to do right."

In an attempt to be more enquiring the reporter stated "You and Medgar Evers fought for the Civil Rights of the African American, for the underprivileged, for freedom that has still not materialised. Ultimately, nothing much has changed despite your best efforts. There are still to this very day riots, hatred of races, prejudice against the underdog, and coloured people being downtrodden. Despite all your best civil rights efforts, amendments to the segregation laws, despite changes to the laws of the land and Bill of Rights, progress has been limited." I could almost hear Medgar Evers the father of the Civil Rights movement in America chime away in a telling statement: "You can kill a man but you can't kill an idea."

On August 28, 1963, Martin Luther King Jr., delivered a speech to a massive group of civil rights marchers gathered around the Lincoln Memorial in Washington DC. The March on Washington for Jobs and Freedom brought together the nation's most prominent civil rights leaders, along with tens of thousands of marchers, to press the United States government for equality. The culmination of this event was the influential and most memorable speech of Dr. King's career. Popularly known as the "I Have a Dream" speech, the words of that speech influenced the Federal government to take more direct actions to fully realize racial equality.

"I am happy to join with you today in what will go down in history as the greatest demonstration for freedom in the history of our nation. Five score years ago, a great American, in whose symbolic shadow we stand today, signed the Emancipation Proclamation. This momentous decree came as a great beacon light of hope to millions of Negro slaves who had been seared in the flames of withering injustice. It came as a joyous daybreak to end the long night of their captivity.

But one hundred years later, the Negro still is not free. One hundred years later, the life of the Negro is still sadly crippled by the manacles of segregation and the chains of discrimination. One hundred years later, the Negro lives on a lonely island of poverty amid a vast ocean of material prosperity. One hundred years later, the Negro is still languished in the corners of American society and finds himself an exile in his land. And so we've come here today to dramatize a shameful condition." "In a sense, we've come to our nation's capital to cash a check. When the architects of our republic wrote the magnificent words of the Constitution and the Declaration of Independence." They were signing a promissory note to which every American was to fall heir. This note was a promise that all men, yes, black men as well as white men, would be guaranteed the "unalienable Rights" of "Life, Liberty and the pursuit of Happiness." It is obvious today that America has defaulted on this promissory note, insofar as her citizens of colour are concerned. Instead of honouring this sacred obligation, America has given the Negro people a bad check, a check which has come back marked "insufficient funds."

"But we refuse to believe that the bank of justice is bankrupt. We refuse to believe that there are insufficient funds in the great vaults of opportunity of this nation. And so, we've come to cash this check, a check that will give us upon demand the riches of freedom and the security of justice. We have also come to this hallowed spot to remind America of the fierce urgency of Now. This is no time to engage in the luxury of cooling off or to take the tranquillising drug of gradualism. Now is the time to make real the promises of democracy. Now is the time to rise from the dark and desolate valley of segregation to the sunlit path of racial justice. Now is the time to lift our nation from the quicksands of racial injustice to the solid rock of brotherhood. Now is the time to make justice a reality for all of God's children."

It would be fatal for the nation to overlook the urgency of the moment. This sweltering summer of the Negro's legitimate discontent will not pass until there is an invigorating autumn of freedom and equality. Nineteen sixty-three is not an end, but a beginning. And those who hope that the Negro needed to blow off steam and will now be content will have a rude awakening if the nation returns to business as usual. And there will be neither rest nor tranquillity in America until the Negro is granted his citizenship rights. The whirlwinds of revolt will continue to shake the foundations of our nation until the bright day of justice emerges.

But there is something that I must say to my people, who stand on the warm threshold that leads into the palace of justice: In the process of gaining our rightful place, we must not be guilty of wrongful deeds. Let us not seek to satisfy our thirst for freedom by drinking from the cup of bitterness and hatred. We must forever conduct our struggle on the high plane of dignity and discipline. We must not allow our creative protest to degenerate into physical violence. Again and again, we must rise to the majestic heights of meeting physical force with soul force.

The marvellous new militancy which has engulfed the Negro community must not lead us to a distrust of all white people, for many of our white brothers, as evidenced by their presence here today, have come to realize that their destiny is tied up with our destiny. And they have come to realize that their freedom is inextricably bound to our freedom.

We cannot walk alone.

And as we walk, we must pledge that we shall always march ahead.

We cannot turn back."

"Some are asking the devotees of civil rights, When will you be satisfied?" We can never be satisfied as long as the Negro is the victim of the unspeakable horrors of police brutality. We can never be satisfied as long as our bodies, heavy with the fatigue of travel, cannot gain lodging in the motels of the highways and the hotels of the cities. **We cannot be satisfied as long as the negro's basic mobility is from a smaller ghetto to a larger one. We can never be satisfied as long as our children are stripped of their self-hood and robbed of their dignity by signs stating: "For Whites Only."** We cannot be satisfied as long as a Negro in Mississippi cannot vote and a Negro in New York believes he has nothing for which to vote. No, no, we are not satisfied, and we will not be satisfied until "justice rolls down like waters, and righteousness like a mighty stream."

"I am not unmindful that some of you have come here out of great trials and tribulations. Some of you have come fresh from narrow jail cells. And some of you have come from areas where your quest -- quest for freedom left you battered by the storms of persecution and staggered by the winds of police brutality. You have been the veterans of creative suffering. Continue to work with the faith that unearned suffering is redemptive. Go back to Mississippi, go back to Alabama, go back to South Carolina, go back to Georgia, go back to Louisiana, go back to the slums and ghettos of our northern cities, knowing that somehow this situation can and will be changed."

" Let us not wallow in the valley of despair, I say to you today, my friends."

"And so even though we face the difficulties of today and tomorrow, I still have a dream. It is a dream deeply rooted in the American dream."

"I have a dream that one day this nation will rise and live out the true meaning of its creed: "We hold these truths to be self-evident, that all men are created equal."

" I have a dream that one day on the red hills of Georgia, the sons of former slaves and the sons of former slave owners will be able to sit down together at the table of brotherhood."

" I have a dream that one day even the state of Mississippi, a state sweltering with the heat of injustice, sweltering with the heat of oppression, will be transformed into an oasis of freedom and justice.

" I have a dream that my four little children will one day live in a nation where they will not be judged by the colour of their skin but by the content of their character. "

" I have a *dream* today!"

" I have a dream that one day, *do*wn in Alabama, with its vicious racists, with its governor having his lips dripping with the words of "interposition" and "nullification" -- one day right there in Alabama little black boys and black girls will be able to join hands with little white boys and white girls as sisters and brothers."I have a *dream* today!

" I have a dream that one day every valley shall be exalted, and every hill and mountain shall be made low, the rough places will be made plain, and the crooked places will be made straight; "and the glory of the Lord shall be revealed and all flesh shall see it together."

" This is our hope, and this is the faith that I go back to the South with."

" With this faith, we will be able to hew out of the mountain of despair a stone of hope. With this faith, we will be able to transform the jangling discords of our nation into a beautiful symphony of brotherhood. With this faith, we will be able to work together, to pray together, to struggle together, to go to jail together, to stand up for freedom together, knowing that we will be free one day."

And this will be the day -- this will be the day when all of God's children will be able to sing with new meaning:

" *My country 'tis of thee, sweet land of liberty, of thee I sing. The land where my fathers died, land of the Pilgrim's pride, From every mountainside, let freedom ring!* "

"And if America is to be a great nation, this must become true. "

" And so let freedom ring from the prodigious hilltops of New Hampshire."

" Let freedom ring from the mighty mountains of New York."

" Let freedom ring from the heightening Alleghenies of Pennsylvania. "

" Let freedom ring from the snow-capped Rockies of Colorado."

" Let freedom ring from the curvaceous slopes of California."

" But not only that:

Let freedom ring from Stone Mountain of Georgia.

Let freedom ring from Lookout Mountain of Tennessee.

Let freedom ring from every hill and molehill of Mississippi.

From every mountainside, let freedom ring."

" And when this happens, and when we allow freedom ring, when we let it ring from every village and every hamlet, from every state and every city, we will be able to speed up that day when *all* of God's children, black men and white men, Jews and Gentiles, Protestants and Catholics, will be able to join hands and sing in the words of the old Negro spiritual:

Free at last! Free at last!

Thank God Almighty, we are free at last!"

"...And then I got into Memphis. And some began to say the threats or talk about the threats that were out. What would happen to me from some of our sick white brothers? Well, I don't know what will happen now. We've got some difficult days ahead. But it doesn't matter to me now, because I've been to the mountaintop. And I don't mind. Like anybody, I would like to live a long life. Longevity has its place. But I'm not concerned about that now. I just want to do God's will.."

"… And He's allowed me to go up to the mountain. And I've looked over. And I've seen the Promised Land. I may not get there with you. But I want you to know tonight, that we, as a people, will get to the promised land! And so I'm happy, tonight. I'm not worried about anything. I'm not fearing any man! My eyes have seen the glory of the coming of the Lord!! "

Shortly after 6 p.m. on April 4, 1968, Dr. Martin Luther King Jr. the day after he made this speech' was shot and mortally wounded as he stood on the second-floor balcony outside his room at the Lorraine Motel in Memphis, Tennessee.

On March 26, 1964, Martin Luther King Jr. and Malcolm X met briefly by chance as they were waiting for a press conference. The two black leaders were on Capitol Hill, attending a Senate debate on the Civil Rights Act of 1964. The differences between them and the movements they represented are often oversimplified in textbooks. The next chapter delves into the difference between the attitude and approach of Malcolm X which is contra to that Of Martin Luther King Jr.'s approach to the issues of Native Americans.

"The good die first, and they whose hearts are dry as summer dust, burn to the socket."

- ——William Wordsworth.

CHAPTER 8.

THE 'X' FACTOR

Malcolm X was a minister, civil rights activist, and prominent Black Nationalist leader who served as a spokesman for the Nation of Islam during the 1950s and 1960s. Due largely to his efforts, the Nation of Islam grew from a mere 400 members at the time he was released from prison in 1952 to 40,000 members in 1960. As the nation's most visible proponent of Black Nationalism, Malcolm X's challenge to the multiracial nonviolent approach of Martin Luther King, Jr; helped set the tone for the ideological and tactical conflicts that took place within the black freedom struggle of the 1960s.

Born in Nebraska, while an infant Malcolm moved with his family to Lansing, Michigan. When Malcolm was six years old, his father, the Rev. Earl Little, a Baptist minister and former supporter of the early Black nationalist leader Marcus Garvey, died after being hit by a streetcar, quite possibly the victim of murder by whites. The surviving family was so poor that Malcolm's mother, Louise Little, resorted to cooking dandelion greens from the street to feed her children. After she was committed to an insane asylum in 1939, Malcolm and his siblings were sent to foster homes or to live with family members.

Malcolm excelled in school, but after one of his eighth-grade teachers told him that he should become a carpenter instead of a lawyer, he lost interest and soon ended his formal education. As a rebellious youngster, Malcolm moved from the Michigan State Detention Home, a juvenile home in Mason, Michigan, to the Roxbury section of Boston to live with an older half-sister, Ella, from his father's first marriage. There he became involved in petty criminal activities in his teenage years. Known as "Detroit

Red" for the reddish tinge in his hair, he developed into a street hustler, drug dealer, and leader of a gang of thieves in Roxbury and Harlem, (in New York City).

While in prison for robbery from 1946 to 1952, he underwent a conversion that eventually led him to join the nation of Islam, an African American movement that combined elements of Islam with Black nationalism. His decision to join the Nation also was influenced by discussions with his brother Reginald, who had become a member in Detroit and who was incarcerated with Malcolm in the Norfolk Prison Colony in Massachusetts in 1948. Malcolm quit smoking and gambling and refused to eat pork in keeping with the Nation's dietary restrictions. To educate himself, he spent long hours reading books in the prison library, even memorizing a dictionary. He also sharpened his forensic skills by participating in debate classes. Following Nation tradition, he replaced his surname, "Little," with an "X," a custom among Nation of Islam followers who considered their family names to have originated with white slaveholders.

After his release from prison, Malcolm helped to lead the Nation of Islam during the period of its greatest growth and influence. He met Elijah Muhammad in Chicago in 1952 and then began organizing temples for the Nation in New York, Philadelphia, and Boston and in cities in the South. He founded the Nation's newspaper, *Muhammad Speaks*, which he printed in the basement of his home, and initiated the practice of requiring every male member of the Nation to sell an assigned number of newspapers on the street as a recruiting and fund-raising technique. He also articulated the Nation's racial doctrines on the inherent evil of whites and the natural superiority of Blacks.

Malcolm rose rapidly to become the minister of Boston Temple No. 11, which he founded; he was later rewarded with the post of minister of Temple No. 7 in Harlem, the largest and most prestigious temple in the Nation after the Chicago headquarters. Recognizing his talent and ability, Elijah Muhammad, who had a special affection for Malcolm, named him the National Representative of the Nation of Islam, second in rank to Muhammad himself. Under Malcolm's lieutenancy, the Nation claimed a membership of 500,000. The actual number of members fluctuated, however, and the influence of the organization, refracted through the public persona of Malcolm X, always greatly exceeded its size.

In 1964 Malcolm X made a decision to break with Muhammad and the Nation of Islam and founded his organisation, This first reinvention saw him become an orthodox Sunni Muslim and reject what he saw as the NOI's insular black nationalism in favour of an engagement with civil rights activism and a broader battle against racism. He visited Britain and spoke at the University of Oxford, addressed heads of state in Cairo, and back in America he created an organisation of Afro-American Unity to advance his evolving perspective perhaps summed up in a new phase 'more African than American.'

Malcolm X's difference from the civil rights mainstream was embodied in a *Life* magazine photo of 1964, in which he clutched a rifle. And his language remained pungent, spiky, and challenging. But his life became increasingly endangered because of hostility not just with white racist groups but from the NOI. In a speech in Detroit on 14th February 1965 he elaborated on his differences with the NOI and on his Afro-American perspective. A week later, he was beginning another of his speeches at his regular venue in New York's Audubon Ballroom. He did not get far before an NOI gunman in the audience shot him dead.

The title of Malcolm X's speech, "The Ballot or the Bullet," suggests an ultimatum between voting or violence, an attempt by the speaker to convince the audience that one action or the other is necessary depending on the actions of the enemy – in this case, the U.S. government.

Before this ultimatum could ever be proposed, however, Malcolm faced the challenge in this speech of establishing a fundamental commonality with his audience. As one of the most prominent members of the Nation of Islam (an African-American religious movement, abbreviated as NOI) and an avid proponent of both separatism and Black nationalism, Malcolm X defined his identity in contrast to members of the Black community who identified as Christian and/or favoured non-violent resistance and racial integration like the followers of Martin Luther King Jr. In March 1964 (a month before giving this speech), Malcolm publicly announced his split from the NOI, leaving his religious status in question.

Instead of ignoring this obvious religious divide between himself and many of his listeners, Malcolm addresses it in the very beginning of his speech, stating plainly and clearly that he remains a Muslim, but that more importantly he is not speaking to the audience as a Muslim; he is coming to the audience as a fighter. By minimising the importance of their difference in religious beliefs and placing a towering emphasis on the struggles they share as members of the Black community, Malcolm effectively seeks to unify his audience while using the second-person tense to directly rally them to his cause. Using that same tactic, Malcolm goes on to unify ideologies regarding the American North and South, making powerful appeals to pathos and utilizing the ethos built atop the foundation of his earlier remarks to erase the division between them (that ethos being his credibility as someone who shares his listeners' struggles despite their differences in religious beliefs). In grouping the North and South, he seeks to obliterate the audience's pre-established the common view that Northern politicians were allies of the Black community while Southern politicians were their enemies. Instead, Malcolm X argues that the North and South are both one entity (the U.S. government), and that the Black community, as one, must fight for justice using either the ballot or the bullet.

" I'm still a Muslim." This lays the foundation for the ethos he invents throughout his speech, signalling to his listeners that he is someone who will speak the truth about himself no matter the social difficulty, and indirectly signalling that he will do the same for all other matters. He then goes on to draw connections to Christian ministers who have also become active in the struggle for civil rights, stating that these ministers do not enter the civil rights movement as ministers, but as fighters. In his list of Christian ministers, he includes Adam Clayton Powell Jr., preacher Milton Galamison, and, most notably, Dr. Martin Luther King Jr., a man whose philosophies of integration and non-violent resistance greatly differed from his own, and an activist with whom Malcolm publicly disagreed.

The use of "we" throughout the speech has the function of not just solidifying his place as one of the audience but solidifying the audience's place as his equal as well. In doing so, Malcolm includes his listeners in his dialogue; even though he is talking to and teaching them, this speech is as much a discussion between himself and them as it is a lesson from teacher to student. Indeed the audio recording, The audience was full of applause, laughter, and exclamation in response to Malcolm's words, certainly suggests that the audience members feel like they are partaking in an equal discussion as well, as opposed to being lectured or talked down to. The use of the second person pronoun "you" serves to place agency directly into the hands of Malcolm's audience, squarely into the lap of the Black community. Instead of using the passive voice to describe the injustices done to the Black community. He used the active voice. Like " The government has failed us and tricked you."

In assigning full agency to both the Black community and the U.S. government/white people, Malcolm does not expand on the suffering that the Black community has experienced, and he does not try to appeal to pathos based on a reality that his audience is already well-aware of.

In Martin Luther King's " I Have a Dream" speech he specifically chooses not to directly accuse white America of wrongdoing; a strategic move to unify His listeners regardless of their race, and to align them with his own belief that integration and nonviolent resistance were solutions to Black America's civil rights issues. Malcolm, on the other hand, states clearly and directly in his speech who is responsible for the situation of Black America, embracing the possibility of inciting feelings of indignation, injustice, and the desire for separation from white America in his audience (the latter feeling the primary difference from the feelings in King's speech). Another interesting example of the philosophical differences between King and Malcolm X is that, at the end of his 'promissory note" metaphor, King states that "We refuse to believe that the bank of justice is bankrupt."

Here, King appeals to the conscience of white America by not only invoking the sacred founding documents but also stating with conviction that, despite the horrific tortures and trauma that African Americans have experienced in the U.S., he refuses to believe that white America and the U.S. government cannot be made to deliver on that long overdue justice. Malcolm, however, expresses a sharply contrasting view of white America's conscience. In the version of "The Ballot or the Bullet" given in Cleveland, Ohio on April 3, 1964, he states the following:

"America's conscience is bankrupt. She lost all conscience a long time ago. Uncle Sam has no conscience. So you're wasting your time appealing to the conscience of a bankrupt man like Uncle Sam". While King's statement shows his belief in both the existence of white America's conscience and the possibility of appealing to it (arguably a necessary prerequisite to believing in the viability of integration and nonviolent resistance), Malcolm makes no such assumptions.

"You and I have never seen democracy; all we've seen is hypocrisy, we see America not through the eyes of someone who has enjoyed the fruits of Americanism, we see America through the eyes of someone who has been the victim of Americanism. We don't see any American dream; we've experienced only the American nightmare. We haven't benefited from America's democracy; we've only suffered from America's hypocrisy."

This passage serves as a segue into convincing his audience to break their affiliation with mainstream U.S. political parties and even indirectly suggests that they separate themselves from the idea that they are one of the indigenous people of America in addition to making appeals to the value of independence, Malcolm also appeals to the value of freedom using history from both the U.S. and around the world to convince his audience to take action. He refers to countries in Africa and Asia that have gained their independence using the philosophy of nationalism, stating that "brown, red, and yellow people in Africa and Asia are getting their independence. They're not getting it by singing 'We Shall Overcome.' No, they are getting it through " Nationalism.".

Fully aware of the Black community's widespread loyalty to the Democratic party, Malcolm then undertakes the task of convincing his audience that the Democrats (associated with the North) and the "Dixiecrats" (a term for some Southern Democrats, known for supporting segregation and opposing civil rights) are part of one entity, one enemy—the U.S. government.

He develops his argument by expanding on a simple fact: the majority of the government is controlled by Democrats, and yet none of the legislative promises made to the Black community during the previous election year have been kept. "The Democrats have been in After declaring that Democrats and "Dixiecrats" are the same, Malcolm says, "Oh, I say you have been misled. You have been had. You have been taken." By using African American Vernacular English (AAVE), a dialect of English spoken by many Black Americans, Malcolm X achieves multiple purposes. For one, he further builds ethos with the audience by speaking in a way that is familiar to them, in a dialect that is (mostly) exclusive to the Black community, indirectly reminding his audience of his credibility. Secondly, this is a humorous move to close whatever distance his previous remarks may have put between him and the audience (and a successful one at that since the audience erupted into laughter and applause at the statement).

After a holy pilgrimage ("hajj") to the city of Mecca, a trip during which Malcolm encountered Muslims of all different colours and ranks, he began to adopt a far more inclusive view of different races, an expansion of his definition of "we." In a letter written to a friend on April 25 (only thirteen days after delivering his "The Ballot or the Bullet" speech), Malcolm discussed his hajj and said that he felt no racial antagonism towards white people for the first time in his life: "I have never before witnessed such sincere hospitality and the practise of true brotherhood as I have seen and experienced during this pilgrimage here in Arabia. What I have seen and experienced.

Tragically, Malcolm was assassinated less than a year later on February 21, 1965. Though the world would never realise the endless potential he possessed, the spirit of Malcolm's words and the deep love he had for his people lived on in the Black Power movement of the 1960s and 1970s, a movement that emphasises "racial pride, economic empowerment, and the creation of political and cultural institutions." The Black Panther Party for Self-Defence (BPP), founded in October 1966 during this movement in the wake of Malcolm's assassination, was the era's "most influential militant black power organization." The foundation of the BPP was the Ten Point Platform and Program created by BPP founders Huey P. Newton and Bobby Seale. While all ten points existed in harmony with Malcolm X's philosophies, none resonated with them more so than: "We want freedom. We want the power to determine the destiny of our Black Community."

Even though Malcolm's ideologies had only just begun to evolve before his death, his message, legacy, and impact had already extended far beyond the Black community. This is perhaps conveyed most effectively by lifelong Japanese-American activist Yuri Kochiyama, who shared a brief but formative friendship with Malcolm in the year before his death. In a concluding statement for an interview conducted in May of 1972, Kochiyama said the following about Malcolm: "Malcolm's life and what he did with it, rising from the muck of enforced poverty to international recognition, is primarily a message to his people – black people in America, Africa, and the diaspora. But the significance of his feat in transforming his life makes him relevant to all humanity. His life is truly a lesson to prove that one can transcend adversity, hate, and lies. Through struggle, he became the symbol of fearlessness against powerful enemies, of commitment to fighting racism in this society, and a motivator to seek truth."

Kochiyama went on to offer the following insight into who Malcolm was as a person: "Malcolm, as a private individual, was as admirable as he was a political figure, leader, and teacher. He was a loving and caring husband and father. He exuded love for humanity and the ordinary people on the street; the children and the elderly; but most of all for the most rejected, degraded, and ghettoised. He was unpretentious, sincere, genuine, and humble. After he returned from Mecca with the title El Hajj Malik Shabazz, his followers asked him, "What shall we call you now?" He responded, "What did you call me before?" They said, "Brother Malcolm." He answered, "Yes, just Brother Malcolm."

Malcolm X's life was a stunning example of perseverance, fearlessness, compassion, and the most fervent dedication to truth and growth, both his own and his people's. He refused to stagnate in the comfort that comes with familiarity, leaving the Nation of Islam when he determined that he could no longer further his own goals within it (Pilgrim), and changing his long-held notions about race and inclusivity upon his hajj to Mecca.] Quote unquote. Malcolm unknowingly stood, unyielding and unafraid, at the vanguard of the Black Power movement, blazing a path for future activists that stands followed and well-trodden even to this day. He was a man of his people, for his people, who had a fantastic love for reading and, above all, an extraordinary commitment to the fight for equality and freedom that will continue to awe and inspire for generations to come. The contra argument to Malcolm X's philosophy and speech was that violence breeds only violence and heartbreak in the end. In Malcolm X's case, it may be said " He who lives by the sword, dies by the sword." Martin Luther King Junior took more of a pacifist approach in his civil rights activism and speeches, and he likewise died like Malcolm X by an assassin's bullet.

CHAPTER 9.

WHEN THE END GAME IS A LIE

This chapter introduces the evil of one man who by his hatred and political goal turned the world to war and death by his skill as an orator of lies and programmes of death and destruction.

Adolf Hitler was born on April 20, 1889, at Braunau am Inn, Austria. He was the founder and leader of the Nazi Party from 1920 to the time of his death 30th April 1945 and became chancellor and Fuhrer of Germany from 1933 to 1945. Hitler's worldview revolved around two concepts: territorial expansion and racial supremacy. Those themes informed his decision to invade Poland, which marked the start of World War 11, as well as the systematic killing of six million Jews and millions of others during the Holocaust. Hitler's father, Alois (born 1837), was illegitimate. For a time he bore his mother's name, Schicklgruber, but by 1876 he had established his family claim to the surname Hitler. Adolf never used any other surname.

After his father retired from the state customs service, Adolf Hitler spent most of his childhood in Lintz the capital of Upper Austria. It remained his favourite city throughout his life and expressed his wish to be buried there. Alois Hitler died in 1903 but left an adequate pension and savings to support his wife and children. Although Hitler feared and disliked his father, he was a devoted son to his mother, who died after much suffering in 1907. With a mixed record as a student, Hitler never advanced beyond a secondary education.. After leaving school, he visited Vienna and then returned to Linz, where he dreamed of becoming an artist. Later, he used the small allowance he continued to draw to maintain himself in Vienna. He wished to study art, for which he had some capability, but he twice failed to secure entry to the

Academy of Fine Arts. For some years he lived a lonely and isolated life, earning a precarious livelihood by painting postcards and advertisements whilst he drifting from one municipal hostel to another. Hitler already showed traits that characterized his later life.

In 1913 Hitler moved to Munich. He had applied for Austrian Military service in February 1914 but was classified as unfit because of inadequate physical vigour. However, when World War 1 broke out, he petitioned Bavarian King Louis 111 to be allowed to serve, and one day after submitting that request, he was notified that he would be permitted to join the 16th Bavarian Reserve Infantry Regiment. After some eight weeks of training, Hitler was deployed in October 1914 to Belgium, where he participated in the First Battle of Ypres. He served throughout the war, was wounded in October 1916, and was gassed two years later near Ypres. He was hospitalized when the conflict ended. During the war, he was continuously in the front line as a headquarters runner; his bravery in action was rewarded with the Iron Cross, Second Class, in December 1914, and the Iron Cross, First Class (a rare decoration for a corporal), in August 1918. He greeted the war with enthusiasm, as a great relief from the frustration and the aimlessness of civilian life. He found discipline and comradeship satisfying which was confirmed in his belief in the heroic virtues of war.

Intent on remaining in the army, having found a real purpose in life. Hitler was appointed to the Military Intelligence Propaganda section where he undertook political training. His activities involved making speeches to the troops advocating German nationalism and non-socialism, where he developed further his oratory skills. He also acted as an army informer, spying on small political parties. He, at the time, joined the German Workers

Party, an extreme anti-Communist, anti-Semitic right-wing organisation.

In 1920 Hitler was discharged from the army. In the German Worker's Party, he undertakes responsibility for publicity and propaganda. He changes the party's name to the National Socialist German Workers Party, (or Nazi for short) The party represents a combination of intense hatred for the politicians whom they considered had dishonoured Germany by signing the Versailles Treaty and exploiting local grievances against a weak federal government.

Hitler challenges Anton Drexler to become the leader of the Nazi party. After initial resistance, Drexler agrees and Hitler becomes the new leader of the party. And in 1923 Along with other right-wing factions and General Ludendorff, he attempted to overthrow the Bavarian government with an armed uprising. The event became known as The Beer Hall Putsch. Hitler and 2000 Nazi's march through Munich to the Beer Hall, to take over a meeting chaired by three of the most important individuals in Bavarian politics. Defendants in the Beer Hall Putsch trial, apart from Hitler included Pernet, Weber, Frick, Krieber, Ludendorff, Brucker, Rohm and Wagner.

The following day, the Nazis march in the streets, the police open fire. Hitler escapes but is captured, tried for treason and serves 9 months in Landsberg prison. It was during his imprisonment that he began dictating his thoughts to Rudolf Hess, which emerged in the book *Mein Kampf* (My Struggle). It is a mixture of autobiography, political ideology and an examination of the techniques of propaganda.

In 1925, in his absence, it became clear that no one else could create a successful ultra-right-wing movement. Upon Hitler's release from prison, he reconstitutes the Nazi Party under his exclusive leadership. The Party did very poorly in elections, but this period allowed Hitler to recruit a small but devoted group of followers, including many who would be leading figures in the

Nazi regime after it came to power. So in 1929 at the start of the world economic depression following the crash of the United States stock market in October 1929 gave Hitler a chance. As unemployment skyrocketed in Germany, voters turned against parties associated with the Weimar Republic. The Nazis score a series of successes in state elections. Hitler benefits from the deep divisions among the other German political parties.

The Communists hope to profit from the Depression. They blame Germany's problems on capitalism, call for a revolution, and refuse to cooperate with any of the other parties. Conservative nationalist parties blame parliamentary democracy and the Versailles treaty for Germany's problems. They hope to use the economic crisis to overturn the constitution and restore an authoritarian system similar to the pre-war monarchy. They see Hitler as a potentially useful ally. The Social Democratic Party is the strongest defender of the democratic system but blames the "bourgeois" pro-capitalist parties for the economic crisis. The Catholic Center party has the greatest weight in the government but has no remedy for the Depression. By contrast, the Nazis offer a simple explanation of the crisis—it's the fault of the Jews—and a simple program for ending it. In national parliamentary elections in September 1930, the Nazis score an unexpected success, winning 18% of the vote and becoming the second-largest party (after the Social Democrats). In early 1932 an unpopular coalition government of the Center Party failed to gain support and an election in July where Hitler ran for president against the celebrated war hero Hindenburg and won 37% of the

votes of democracy in Germany; 37% of the vote, whilst the Communists get 16%.

No majority coalition in favour of democracy can be established. Various politicians compete with each other to create a government that will rule by decree. Hitler was offered a place in one of these schemes, engineered by von Schleicher in August 1932, but refused because he would not have full control. The elections are held in November to break the deadlock. For the first time since 1929, the Nazis' share of the vote goes down, to 32%. Fearing that his moment may be about to pass. Hitler became more conciliatory to Schleicher, On January 30, 1933, an agreement was announced. Hitler was named Chancellor (prime minister). Despite the broad support for the Nazis, the party will have only four seats in the cabinet. Schleicher and other conservatives expect Hitler's extremism to undermine his popularity; they will then be able to dismiss him and keep power themselves. It was the Great Depression that created the conditions in which Hitler could come to power; although his party did become the largest in Germany, Hitler was not elected to office; the Nazis never won an absolute majority of votes, even in the final elections held after they came to power in March 1933; Hitler became Chancellor thanks to the calculations of right-wing nationalist politicians who thought they could use his popularity to destroy the Weimar system. Hitler of course had other ideas once he gained control.

Adolf Hitler was completely wrong about absolutely everything..usually. When Hitler said something correctly, it was merely to set up the next lie. As with all good propagandists—and he certainly was that—he would begin with a few obvious, documented facts, and then proceed to distort them horribly. At any rate, the infamous German Führer's worm-tongue rhetoric is 'not' to be taken seriously, except as a classic example of the sort of masterful demagoguery from which appropriate lessons may hopefully, be learned. Here is an extract from his speech to the German Hitler youth in September 1935. Already he has a master plan to eventually use them in war as reserve forces for front-line fighting that ultimately resulted in the loss of many thousands of their lives.

"German Youth! For the third time, you have assembled for this parade, over 50,000 representatives of a community that is growing larger year by year. The importance of those you represent here each year has constantly increased. Not just in terms of numbers; no, we see it here, in terms of value. When I think back to our first parade and the second and compare today's parade with those, I see the same development that we can see in all other aspects of German national life today. Our People are becoming visibly more disciplined, fit and trim, and our youth is beginning to follow this lead. The idea of what a man should be has not always been the same even among our People. There were times - they seem to be long ago and we can scarcely understand them when the ideal young German was the young fellow who could handle his beer and his liquor.

Today, I can say with joy that we no longer idealize the young fellow who can handle his beer and liquor but the young man who can face any weather, the tough young man. For what matters is not merely how many glasses of beer he can drink, but how many blows he can withstand, not how many nights he can spend doing the rounds of the bars and pubs but how many kilometres he can march. Today the German People's ideal is no longer your average beer-drinker but the young men and girls who are fit and trim."

In the same month of September 1935, he gave a short speech at Nuremberg:" Nothing is possible unless one will commands, a will which has to be obeyed by others, beginning at the top and ending at the very bottom. This is the expression of an authoritarian state of a weak, babbling democracy an authoritarian state where everyone is proud to obey because he knows: I will likewise be obeyed when I take command."

To justify the annexation of Austria on 8th April 1938 Hitler called a public vote on whether the unification of Austria and Germany would stand. This is an excerpt from the speech he gave the day before the vote.

"When one day we shall be no more than the coming generation shall be able to look back with pride upon this day, the day in which a great Volk affirmed the German community. In the past millions of German men shed their blood for this Reich. How merciful a fate to be allowed to create this Reich today without suffering. Now, rise. German Volk, subscribe to it, hold it tightly in your hands! I wish to thank Him who allowed me to return to my homeland so that I could return it to my German Reich! May every German realise the importance of the hour tomorrow. Asses and then bow his head in reverence before the will of the Almighty who has wrought this miracle for all of us within these past few weeks. "

Hitler took Austria without shedding blood but it was not so when he took Poland. Just the week before the launching of the attack on Poland, Hitler made an address to the Chief Commanders, at Obsersalzberg, on 22 August 1939.

"Our strength consists in our speed and our brutality. Genghis Khan led millions of women and children to slaughter with premeditation and a happy heart. History sees in him solely the founder of a state. It's a matter of indifference to me what a weak Western European civilisation will say about me. I have issued the command and I'll have anybody who utters but one word of criticism executed by a firing squad that our war aim does not consist in reaching certain lines, but in the physical destruction of the enemy. Accordingly, I have placed my death-head formation in readiness – for the present only in the East – with orders to them to send to death mercilessly and without compassion, men, women, and children of Polish derivation and language. Only thus shall we gain the living space which we need. Who, after all, speaks today of the annihilation of the Armenians?'

Hitler in April 1945 wrote to his command his last order to read to the soldiers on the German Eastern Front; it was his last lie. He had almost deceived himself in believing: " The Jewish Bolshevik arch-enemy has gone over to the attack with his masses for the last time. He attempts to smash Germany and eradicate our nation. You soldiers from the east today already know yourselves to a large extent what fate is threatening, above all, German women, girls and children. While old men and children are being murdered, women and girls are humiliated to the status of barracks prostitutes. Others are marched off to Siberia. We have anticipated this thrust, and since January of this year, everything has been done to build up a strong front. Mighty artillery is meeting the enemy. Our infantry's casualties were replenished by countless new units. Reserve units, new formations and the Volkssturm reinforce our front. This time the Bolsheviks will experience Asia's old fate. That is, he must and will bleed to death in front of the capital of the German Reich.

Whosoever does not do his duty at this moment is a traitor to our nation. The regiment or division that leaves its position acts so disgracefully that it will have to be ashamed before the women and children who are withstanding the bombing terror in our towns. Above all, look out for the treacherous few officers and soldiers who, to secure their own miserable lives, will fight against us in Russian pay, perhaps even in German uniform. Whosoever gives you a command to retreat is, unless you know him well, to be arrested immediately, and if necessary to be executed immediately, irrespective of his rank. "

If in these coming days and weeks, every soldier on the Eastern Front fulfils his duty, Asia's last onslaught will collapse just as in the end our enemies' penetration in the West will despite everything, come to naught. Berlin remains German, Vienna will again be German and Europe will never be Russian. By forming one community, sworn to defend not a vain conception of fatherland, but to defend your homeland, your women, your children and thus your future.

In this hour the entire German nation looks to you, my soldiers in the east, and only hopes that by your fanaticism, by your arms and by your leadership, the Bolshevik onslaught is drowned in a blood bath. At the moment when fate has taken the greatest war criminal of all times from this earth, the war will take a decisive turn".

(Signed) ADOLF HITLER

In the final hours of the war, Hitler's propaganda machine was still in modus operandi, despite many of his commanders and troops surrendering to the Allies. Many of the German people receiving word of the atrocities of the concentration camps believed Hitler was unaware of what was happening, They to the last month of the war believed Hitler's lies.

Even today some speak of the might of the Nazi machine, the turning of the economy around before, during and after the economic depression which had already started in Germany in 1922, well before the 'Black Friday' 1929 Stock market crash and its aftermath. The consequence of economic hardship after the war was felt hard on the German people and many were starving well into the beginning of the 1950s.

Still, some speak with pride of the Nazi-built Autobahn road network that runs through the heart of Germany, the brilliance of the well-oiled train network that is still second to none, the finest in the world. They too look with the pride of the nation when Hitler's commitment to providing families with a cheap German-made car. The Volkswagen-the people's car, founded in 1937 by the German labour front under the Nazi Party and revived into a global brand as it is known today post World War 11, it is known from the ironic Beetle and serves as the flagship of the Volkswagen Group, the largest automotive manufacturer by world standards.

These great achievements fall under the shadow of the death of millions whose blood washes away any grand notion of what was achieved under Adolf Hitler and the Third Reich.

CHAPTER 10

THE GENIUS WHO TAPPED WORLD VIBRATIONS

When one gains the power of tapping into the universal vibrations to achieve great things for the benefit of others then that man can be called quite rightly a genius. Only one man by natural order was capable of doing just that in the 20th century, that man was Nikola Tesla.

Nikola Tesla, it is reported, was born in 1856 to a Serbian family in the then-Austrian Empire which is modern-day Croatia. My Serbian friend Dannie was most keen to share his knowledge on my enquiry into Tesla's parentage and he was emphatic in his belief Tesla's parents were both Serbian and that he was born in Serbia. It turned out that Dannie's knowledge of Tesla was passed on to him by his now-deceased father when Dannie was a young boy. Not wish to doubt my friend who had great admiration for the inventive nature of Tesla and the fact that he seemed to be, in Dannie's opinion, an enlightened spirit who was on a different dimensional plane even when he was here in this world. Dannie had already canonised him a Saint, so I needed to dig a little deeper in another direction to get another viewpoint. Turning to Croatian friend Mirjana over a coffee the very next day, I broached the subject having already explained Dannie's viewpoint about the "Serbian" genius. Mirjana was able to confirm that Nikola Tesla was definitely of Serbian parentage but was born in the mountainous area of the Balkan Peninsula, which is in modern-day Croatia.

During Tesla's early childhood, the Empire was governed by the Austrian monarchy. It was later governed as a dual monarchy in 1856 between Austria and Hungary, the Austro-Hungarian Empire. Of course, these historical facts meant little to a young boy in the mountain terrain of the Balkan Peninsula back then. Nikola didn't inherit his far-sighted genius from his parents. Tesla's father was a stern but loving Orthodox priest who was a gifted writer and poet. Tesla's mother managed the family farm and was a loving happy homebody. A tragic accident, when his brother Daniel was killed in a riding accident shocked an unsettled 7-year-old Nikola. He escaped into study and went on to graduate in maths and physics in his early 20s from the Technical University of Graz and then philosophy at Prague.

It was in 1882, while on a walk, he came up with the idea of a brushless AC motor, making a sketch of rotating electromagnets in the sand on his path. Later that year he moved to Paris working in direct flow current with Continental Edison. Two years later he immigrated to the United States and was hired as an engineer for Thomas Edison's Manhattan headquarters. He worked there for a year, impressing Edison with his diligence and ingenuity. At one point Edison told Tesla he would pay him $50,000 for an improved design for workable DC dynamos. After much experimentation, Tesla presented Edison with a solution and asked for his money. Edison was reluctant to pay and responded: "Tesla, you don't understand American humour." It was not long after that encounter that Tesla quit.

I had a majority of facts on Tesla but needed to dwell a little more deeply on Edison. He was in his lifetime a typical entrepreneurial American of stature. Born in 1847 as the youngest of seven children to Samuel and Nancy Edison. His father was an exiled political activist from Canada who helped support his large family in Milan, Ohio by working as a shopkeeper and sometimes shingle maker. His Wife Nancy a school teacher home-schooled Thomas as he proved not a particularly bright student. He was however very enterprising, selling vegetables,
candy and newspapers on trains. His family moved to Port Huron, Michigan where Thomas spent much of his childhood. He

secured work at the height of the stock market rally as a ticker tape reader. The ticker tape machine was called a stock ticker which printed abbreviated company names as alphabetic symbols followed by numeric stock transactions, prices and volume information. The term 'ticker' came from the sound made by the machine as it printed. Since there were hundreds of companies being traded and prices updated every minute, it meant the whole stream of information was being held up, so the company names were reverted to symbols.

Edison could read the continual flow of ticker tape symbols at lightning speed and report his findings to his employer, while fellow staff members were still trying to keep up with the market. He was often seen with his feet up on a desk drinking his coffee and staring at his fellow employees with amusement at the pace they read the machine reports. He spent much of his spare time coming up with patentable ideas, be they his own or what he could get for nothing from other people's brainwaves. Whilst in his lifetime he patented 1,093 ideas and became the driving force behind the innovation of the photograph, the incandescent light bulb and the motion picture camera it was more the work of the genius of others as his employees that he tapped into, in that you might call him a genius.

He also created the world's first industrial research laboratory, setting it up on an unsuccessful real estate development site called Menlo Park. It was within a community location within Edison's township of Middlesex County, New Jersey. He cunningly set it up as an unincorporated community business model which faired well for him tax-wise and he encouraged many inventories and men with smart ideas to come and work for him. He had no moral compulsion to patent their ideas in his
name and justified it all as they were in his employ at the time. Edisons was a performer of conjuring tricks that earned him the title; " Wizard of Menlo Park." He rose to great heights of fame

and wealth as electricity spread around the world. Edison's various electric companies continued to grow until in 1889 they were brought together to form Edison General Electric, which we simply know by its brand " GE."

Like so many workable inventions the masses usually end up with the rough end of the pineapple and electricity in that regard was no exception. Edison stole Tesla's ideas and when Edison was challenged with a far superior alternative current (AC) by Tesla, which was better and more efficient, he marketed and sold his direct current, as he was more adept in the marketplace than Tesla. It went to court and the so-called " Battle of the Currents" resulted in a win for Edison who convinced the jury that Tesla's AC was dangerous. In his polyphase AC motor, Tesla scored a victory over Edison. The public took to the methodology of direct current on wires as the preferred method of providing cheap electricity. Edison had put it out there that micro technology for proving electricity had great risks, as he had done in court. He was a born marketeer and raconteur, as with all his inventions, be they originating from him or taken from another, he was prepared to do anything possible to win. Edison, on the back of creating a way to charge money for electricity, controlled energy resources. Although a philanthropist, he only gave money in areas that would benefit him in the long run. Nikola Tesla invented and created renewable energy and cared more for people than making money. Edison died with $12,000 in his bank account while Tesla died penniless. Both men certainly changed the face of the modern world with their inventions.

While Edison had some 1093 patents at the time of his death., Tesla was responsible for over 700 patents of which 278 patented inventions are in use today. There is some speculation that Tesla's patents continue to come to light long after his death. The likes of the mobile phone, and basic discoveries like radio, robotics and computer science are all credited to man. He was known as the man who caused lightning to strike by harnessing energy from a basic triangle and demonstrated this happening.

It was after the bombing of Pearl Harbour that Tesla contacted the US Military advising he had invented a 'death ray," that could melt the engine in an approaching aircraft some 40 miles away with microwaves. He reportedly died that night and military personnel turned up to take away a chest full of patentable ideas which are slowly being released to the public as the authorities see fit to do so. Tesla was probably murdered for his creations to ensure they would not fall into the wrong hands and could then be under military control or as we know, some big business of the day held.

We may never know for certain but more and more Tesla inventions are surprising us in our modern world now. Possibly his electromagnetic field dynamo alternative current grid which has now been adopted to use in such everyday uses as washing machines, electricity generators and modern motor cars to name but a few is best known. He also came up with the best-known fuel-based solutions to world energy and spoke as a green environmentalist on the best method to clean up the needless use of fossil fuels over a century ago.

It was not until after he died in his hotel room in 1943 that the Supreme Court voided four of Marconi's key patents, accrediting Tesla's innovation on radio transmission. The AC system however that he championed and improved remains the global
standard for power transmission even today. The TV towers and cell links for mobiles were another of his patents that were realised for manufacture long after his death. He also invented electric oscillators, and meters and improved light and high-quality transformers with his Tesla coil. He had demonstrated his invention of the X-ray and gave short demonstrations of his radio communication two years before Marconi came on the scene.

Together with Westinghouse he lit the 1891 World Columbian Exposition in Chicago and partnered up with his old rival, Edison's GE to install AC generators at Niagara Falls creating the world's first modern power station.

Tesla, a futurist had said in his time on earth that the 20th and 21st century was born in his head. We celebrate conversely the magnetic field and sing hymns to your induction engine. We marvel at the way he caught the light from the depth of the earth and created fire in the heavens. There he also created a weapon that causes earthquake vibrations and discovered cosmic rays. It has followed that races of people will continue singing his praises in the temple of the future, because of the great secret that certain elements can be watered with life forces from ether. Now what would Tesla say to that? "Yes, these are some of my most important discoveries. I'm a defeated man. I have accomplished the greatest thing I could."What now is it then Mr. Tesla, what of your dreams when you were cut off from life before your time? Tesla may have well replied: "I wanted to illuminate the whole earth. There is enough electricity here to become a second sun. Light would then appear around the equator, like the rings around Saturn."

He once stated "Mankind is still not ready for the great and good. In Colorado Springs I soaked the earth with electricity. Also, we can water the earth with other energies, such as positive mental energy. They are already in the music of Bach or Mozart and you heard it in the fiery music of my deaf friend Beethoven and you have heard it in the verses of the poets. In the earth's interior, there are energies of joy, peace and love. They express themselves in flowers that grow on the earth, in the food we partake of and in everything that makes man's homeland. I've spent years looking for the way that energy could influence people. The beauty and the secret of roses are as medicine and the rays of the sun are food."

" Life has an infinite number of forms, and Science must find in every form the matter. Three things are essential in this. And all man has to do is search for them. I know I didn't find them but don't you give up, let no man give up on them. I knew that gravity is proven if one needs to fly but it was not my intention to make flying devices for transport nor weapons of war, but to teach individuals to regain consciousness on their wings. I am trying still to awaken the energy contained in the air. That may be the main source of energy. What you consider as space is a manifestation of matter that is not yet awakened. There is no space on earth, nor in the Universe in black holes, what astronomers talk about are the most powerful sources of powerful energy and life."

He had gone on to say. "One issue is food. We need a stellar of terrestrial energy to feed the hungry on earth. With wine in limited intake, we can cheer our hearts and understand that there is the God of the universe and other Gods beneath that power too. The power of evil is man's greatest destroyer and suffering continues as man's life passes. These evil outcomes do not come from God, they are of a different order in space. It is an evil that man sometimes taps into to create great epidemics, one of which you may experience worldwide. (He may have been referring to Covid-19?) In this century the disease has spread from the Earth now throughout the whole Universe. The other is that there is excess light in the Universe I discovered a star that by all astronomic and mathematical laws could disappear and nothing would seem to be modified. This star is in this galaxy. Its light can occur in such density that it fits into a sphere smaller than an apple, and is heavier than our Solar System."

"Religions and philosophers teach that man can become the Christ, Buddha and Zoroaster. What I'm eluding to is trying to improve something wilder and almost unattainable. This is what to do in the Universe now so that every being is born as Christ, Buddha or Zoroaster."

It was far beyond my imagination what Tesla was proposing, but I get the power of manifestation in allowing one's Higher Power (self) to live according to the divine will and not one's own. It gave me pause for thought to attempt more often to hand over my earthly needs and desires to the will of the Almighty, but I knew that when my free will gets in the way it makes it almost impossible for me and by all accounts my friend the Inventor. I made a mental note of the three elements Tesla alluded to. 1. The issue of food. 2- The issue of good over evil and 3- The harnessing of the excess light in the Universe.

I could now see that rather than discuss Mr Edison's inventions, it was entirely possible to keep the focus on the theme set by Tesla. It had dawned on me that we have all the benefits now of the inventions of both men and that what we need now is guidance to take our duty on earth to the next level. A spiritual invention if you will. I could see that Tesla had tapped my thoughts and was keen to see what his friend would say. He made it a little easier by stating: "An inventor's endeavour is essentially life-saving, be it whether he harnesses forces, improves devices, provides new comforts and conveniences, to the safety of existence.

In my mind's eye too, I could hear Tesla again; " It mattered little to me if my creations were stolen as long as they proved beneficial to man, and that the ones who stole didn't give up on their ideas." Edison may well have drawn on his ability to get things done. His right of reply he may well have said: "The first requirement is the awareness of our mission, the second condition to adapt too is a determination to continue, that one might finish the task." "This is guidance from all vital and spiritual energy in labour. Man will gain not lose in this undertaking,"

I remember Tesla once talking about the maintenance of the assembly. It dawned on me then and there that he was talking about the human body being a perfect machine. Knowing the circuitry of the body and what is good for it, he pointed out that most people eat foods that are harmful to the body and those who cook should touch their hands before proceeding. "Adjust to your physical circuit, in addition to food, dreaming is important even when you're wide awake." He had trained himself to live sometimes on one hour sleep per day which required superhuman effort to achieve his daily creative goals. He had indicated he gained the ability to fall asleep and wake up at a designated time to return to his tasks at hand. "If into something I do not understand I force myself in my dreams to thus find a solution."

Tesla indicated that light particles of energy are all around us and if we meditate upon this phenomenon and consume it in the now, then what we see, hear, read and learn allows us to accomplish geniuses from these particles of light that are obedient and faithful to our bidding. I had been very mindful of the art of visualisation in my mind's eye as I created and wrote books, poems and songs. The events that I visualise are real in front of my eyes, visualising as each occurrence manifests. I understand now how Tesla (and maybe Edison to some degree) harnessed the power to use exceptional gifts and talent. Tesla indeed nurtured it,

guarded the gifts, made corrections to the visualisation of most of his inventions and finished them all with some complex mathematical equations. His abilities were beyond me but I could see now in my small way that to make my creative effort more effective I needed to call on the efforts of other humans in my limitations.

I had made a preemptive judgement on Edison's character, and so didn't not give him as much attention as Tesla. Perhaps on reflection, they exposed more defects of my character in taking his inventory than the 'sins' of such a prominent and inventive genius. So much of what I take for granted in my everyday living was provided by those men of genius. Why even the light I was working under came from the brain of Edison and the computer I now type on and communicate with via the World Wide Web was initially the brainchild of Tesla. As early as 1900 he began to build a global communication network centred on a giant tower at Wardencliffe, on Long Island. If J.P. Morgan, the great finance broker had not balked at Tesla's grandiose scheme for a worldwide communication network, we may well have had the benefit of his radio, television and computer technology much sooner had J.P. Morgan not ceased to finance these ideas.

Tesla lived his last decades in a New York hotel, working on new inventions even as his energy and mental health faded. His obsession with the number three and its multiplication and algorithmic combinations and his fastidious 'washing' of electric current were dismissed as the eccentricities of a genius. In his final years, he claimed communication with the city's pigeons. Tesla died in his room on January 7th, 1943.

Thomas Edison is considered one of history's greatest inventors. He is credited with developing the light bulb, the phonograph and the motion picture camera, among many others. He is credited with a world record of 1093 patents which he held both singly and jointly. On the 50th anniversary of Edison's electric light in 1929, Henry Ford reconstructed Edison's invention factory as a museum at Greenfield Village, Michigan, which he opened. The main celebration of Light's Golden Jubilee, co-hosted by Henry Ford and General Electric, took place in Dearborn along with a huge celebratory dinner in Edison's honour attended by notables such as President Hoover, and John. D. Rockefeller, Jr., George

Eastman, Marie Curie, and Orville Wright. Edison's health however had declined to the point that he could not stay for the entire ceremony. For the last two years of his life, a series of ailments caused a decline in his health even more until he collapsed into a coma; he died on October 18th, 1931.

"Let the future tell the truth and evaluate each one according to his work and accomplishments. The present is theirs; the future, for which I worked, is mine." "The scientists of today think deeply instead of clearly. One must be sane to think clearly, but one can think deeply and be quite insane."

—- Nikola Tesla

CHAPTER 11

THE DANGERS OF INDIFFERENCE

On April 19th, 1999, President Bill Clinton, First Lady Hillary Clinton and members of Congress gathered at the White House's East Room. As part of a Millennium series of Talks, theory wee thereto hear a man speak about the past, the present and the future. The central theme of the speech and its title was ' the perils of indifference', and the speaker had more authority than most to warn of the dangers. His name- Eliezer Wiesel.

In brief, Eliezer "Elie" Wiesel was a Romanian-born American writer, professor, political activist, Nobel laureate, and Holocaust survivor. He authored 57 books, written mostly in French and English, including Night, a work based on his experiences as a Jewish prisoner in the Auschwitz and Buchenwald concentration camps in 1944 and was a Holocaust survivor.

Wiesel was only 15 years old when the Nazis deported him and his family to Auschwitz-Birkenau. His mother and younger sister died in the gas chambers on the night of their arrival at Auschwitz-Birkenau. He and his father were deported to Buchenwald where his father died before the camp was liberated on April 11, 1945. Wiesel's mother and one sister were killed in Nazi death chambers. His father died of starvation and dysentery in the Buchenwald camp. His siblings Beatrice and Hilda survived the war and were reunited with Wiesel at a French orphanage. They eventually emigrated to North America, with Beatrice moving to Montreal, Quebec, Canada. Siblings Tzipora, Shalom, and Sarah did not survive the Holocaust.

After the war, Mr Wiesel lived in a French orphanage and went on to become a journalist. Elie moved to live in the United States of America, married and had a son. He gave his son the name Shalom, the same name as his father.

Apart from the many books he wrote, He did a lot of work to tell people about what the Nazis did to Jews. Elie Wiesel died at his Manhattan home on July 2, 2016 age 87 years.

After years of silence about his wartime experience, and the promotion of the French intellectual Francois Muriac, he finally put pen to paper, bolting down a long narrative into a slim 1985 memoir, lo Nuit. It appeared in English as the Night (1960) and grew into a global phenomenon and one of the cornerstones of Holocaust literature. He followed this with many more novels L'Aude (Dawn) and Le Jour (Day). and further memoirs. But it was 'Night' that propelled Wiesel into the role of public voice of authority on humanitarian issues, a role that earned him the Nobel Peace Prize in 1986 and which saw the creation of the Elie Wiesel Foundation to combat indifference, intolerance and injustice.

On that 12th April 1999 morning in the East Room of the White House, Hillary Clinton introduced Wiesel by saying: 'You have taught us never to forget. You have made sure that we always listen to the victims of indifference, hatred and evil Wiesel's message was a simple but profound one: that indifference and lack of action become allies of evil. As he described it.' In the place I come from, society was composed of three simple categories, the killers, the victims, and the bystanders.'

By contrast, he remembered the US soldiers who liberated him from Buchenwald, to whom he would 'always be grateful' for their righteous rage at what they found. And, moving from the past to the present, he welcomed the 1999 intervention by NATO in Kosovo, against Serbian forces who were attempting to cleanse the region of its ethnically Albanian population. For Wiesel, the dangers of indifference must always persist, but so must the means to avoid them. He concluded that 'we walk towards the new millennium, carried by profound fear and extraordinary hope.'

'We are on the threshold of a new century, a new millennium. What will the legacy of the vanishing century be? How will it be remembered in the new millennium? Surely it will be judged, and judged severely, in both moral and metaphysical terms. These failures have cast a dark shadow over humanity; two world wars, countless civil wars, and the senseless chain of assassinations (Gandhi. Kennedys, Martin Luther King, Sadat, Rabin), bloodbaths in Cambodia and Nigeria, India Pakistan, Ireland, and Rwanda, Eritrea and Ethiopia, Sarajevo and Kosovo, the inhumanity in the gulag and the tragedy of Hiroshima and Nagasaki. And, on a different level, of course, Auschwitz and Treblinka. So much violence, so much indifference.

What is indifference? Etymologically, the word means no difference. A strange and unnatural state in which the lines blur between light and darkness, dusk and dawn, crime and punishment, cruelty and compassion, good and evil. Is it a philosophy of conceivable indifference? Can one possibly view indifference as a virtue? Is it necessary at times to practise it simply to keep, one's sanity, and live normally? Enjoy a fine meal and a glass of wine, as the world around us experiences harrowing up-heaves.

Of course, indifferences can be tempting- more than that, seductive. It is so much easier to look away from victims. It is so much easier to avoid such rude interruptions to our work, our dreams and our hopes. It is, after all, awkward, and troublesome, to be involved in another person's pain and despair. Yet, for the indifferent person, his or her neighbours are of no consequence. And, therefore, their lives are meaningless. Their hidden or even visible anguish is of no interest. Indifference reduces the other to abstraction.

In a way, to be different to that suffering is what makes the human being inhuman. Indifference, after all, is more dangerous than anger and hatred. Anger can at times be creative. One writes a poem, a great symphony: One does something special for the sake of humanity because one is angry at the injustice that one witnesses. But indifference is never creative. Even hatred at times may elicit a response, You fight at. You denounce it. You disarm it.

Indifference elicits no response Indifference is not a beginning, it's an end. And, therefore, indifference is always the friend of the enemy, for it benefits the aggressor- never the victim, whose pain is magnified when he or she feels forgotten. The political prisoner in his cell, the hungry children, the homeless refugee-not to respond to their plight, not to relieve their solitude by offering them a spark of hope is to exile them from human memory. And in denying their humanity, we betray our own. Indifference, then, is not only a sin, it is a punishment. And that is one of the most important lessons of this outgoing century's ranging experiments in good and evil."

Wiesel received numerous awards for his literary and human rights activities. These include the Presidential Medal of Freedom, the U.S. Congressional Gold Medal the Medal of Liberty Award and the rank of Grand Officer in the French Legion of Honour. President Jimmy Carter appointed Wiesel chairman of the United States Holocaust Memorial Council in 1978. In 1986, Elie Wiesel won the Nobel Prize for Peace. Shortly thereafter, Elie Wiesel and his wife established The Elie Wiesel Foundation for Humanity.

Wiesel had defended the cause of Soviet Jews, Nicaragua's Miskito Indians, Argentina's "disappeared," Cambodian refugees, the Kurds, South African apartheid victims, famine victims in Africa and more recently the victims and prisoners in the former Yugoslavia.

In presenting the Nobel Peace Prize, Egil Aarvik, chair of the Nobel Committee, said this about Wiesel: "His mission is not to gain the world's sympathy for victims or the survivors. His aims to awaken our conscience. Our indifference to evil makes us partners in the crime. This is the reason for his attack on indifference and his insistence on measures aimed at preventing a new Holocaust. We know that the unimaginable has happened. What are we doing now to prevent it from happening again?"

I wonder now what Elie Wiesels' thoughts would be on indifference to wars in the present millennium of the 21st century.

A major new survey in 2023 by the global think tank said that the average level of "global peacefulness" had sunk for the ninth year in a row, with conflict deaths topping the previous global peak reached in 2014 during the Syrian Civil War. The dramatic increase in death rates was mostly driven by the war in Ukraine, where 83,000 people were killed in the past year, though the bloodiest conflict was in Ethiopia, where 100,000 people lost their lives. The conflicts in Yemen and Syria have now been raging for 9 and 12 years respectively, and in neither is there any apparent prospect of a military victory.

"Even the best-equipped militaries in the world find it difficult to beat a local population that doesn't want to be invaded and is well-resourced, it is down to the sophistication and availability of modern weaponry, which is making asymmetric warfare increasingly easy to continue." Almost anyone with basic engineering training can now detonate bombs remotely, while guns have much more accuracy," the Global Report said.

The report also points out that the number of non-state groups using drones doubled between 2018 and 2022, and the total number of drone strikes nearly tripled over the same period.

A positive trend is development in the Middle East and North Africa over the last three years, 13 countries have improved their peacefulness, and only 7 have deteriorated. Notwithstanding the current war in the Middle East when Hamas, the Palestinian militant group launched an unprecedented assault on Israel on 7th October last, with hundreds of gunmen infiltrating communities near the Gaza Strip. The fighting has sparked up there time and again throughout history, and it is hoped that peace may be restored soon there too.

The biggest improvement in its peacefulness is particularly exemplified by Libya, which for the second year in a row has shown. Although the security situation is still fragile in Libya, the ceasefire signed in 2020 between the Government of National Accord and the Libyan National Army has significantly stabilized the country.

Another positive note was that many countries have become safer internally: Several countries in the Caribbean and Central America, for example, recorded reductions in domestic terrorism and murder rates over the past year.

One of the starkest findings of a report on the economic cost of war stated: "In total, war and violence cost the world $17.5 trillion last year, or 12.9% of global GDP. For those countries most affected by conflict, the impact is particularly devastating:

Ukraine, for instance, spent 63% of its GDP on defence against the Russian invasion."

The threat of future conflict is also startling: The report calculated that a potential Chinese blockade of Taiwan, for instance, would lead to a drop in global economic output equivalent to double the loss that occurred as a result of the 2008 global financial crisis.

"Of course, many arms companies also make money from war, but if that money could be used for stimulating business, or international health in countries suffering disease and poverty, it would have a far more productive benefit for all. Where there is war, there is no peace. However, the absence of war in a given place does not always mean that there is peace. Peace is understood here as a process in which the absence of war is the beginning of a path. War and violence will not lead to peace, as history has shown us. True peace can only be achieved through a transformation of consciousness. Spiritual thinking and living are necessary for this transformation."The usual strategies suggested by political scientists and international relations experts to prevent war include arms control and diplomacy. Approaches to arms control and diplomacy vary in their actual and potential effectiveness. They extend to poverty, infectious disease and environmental degradation; war and violence within States; the spread and possible use of nuclear, radiological, chemical and biological weapons; terrorism; and transnational organized crime.

Achieving a world without war requires a multidimensional approach encompassing various aspects of our global society. From redirecting defence budgets to engaging in virtual diplomacy, promoting education for peace, and addressing environmental challenges, each endeavour plays a role in realizing this feasible dream. By adopting a holistic perspective, nurturing grassroots movements, and embracing diplomacy, we can pave the way for a future where peaceful coexistence prevails. Let us embark on this journey together, for a world without war is not an elusive fantasy, but a tangible reality waiting to be shaped by our collective efforts.

CHAPTER 12.

IN CONCLUSION

This book was written to examine the tenets-principles or doctrines held to be true by famous and infamous people whose influence on humanity turned out to be for the better or worse in terms of their actions on their doctrine of belief. It is interesting to note that their character of spiritual good or evil intent has had an influence on the philosophy and actions of the masses to this very day.

As this book evolved I noted that to a man each suffered much in the moulding of their character to create what they applied of their nature and natural talent to influence humanity.

Our world today is more complex than ever and often overwhelming. We must not let prejudice economic difficulties or complexities overwhelm us. You the reader know deep down the profound impact you can have on changing the course of any challenging situation for the better. You have seen this in the stories of people's lives within the pages of this book Each of us has a unique talent that is woven into the fabric of what makes up society at large. Our actions on any course that is for the betterment of our fellowman, no matter how small contribute to the larger picture.

As D. Rajdeep, Global Modern Learning Champion said in October 2023, in a paper on 'The Power of Individual Action- what we do shapes our world': "Our actions define us and contribute to our personal growth. When we challenge ourselves, step out of our comfort zones, and embrace new experiences, we not only learn but also discover our hidden potential. It's through these actions that we evolve and become better versions of ourselves. The interactions we have and the actions we take significantly impact the relationships we form. Building genuine connections with others is fundamental to personal and professional success. Our actions, such as active listening, empathy, and support, play a crucial role in fostering these relationships.

When we engage in acts of service, volunteering, or advocating for causes we believe in we can drive positive change in our communities and beyond. Each small effort contributes to a larger movement for social good."

" No matter how humble our work may be, our actions in our workplace play a significant role in our success and those of others if you can see the bigger picture. Our work ethic, collaboration with others, and commitment to continuous improvement directly influence our career trajectory and possibly that of others too. It's the small daily actions that add up to long-term achievements.

Being proactive, taking on new challenges, and maintaining a positive attitude can set us apart in our careers. Consistently delivering high-quality work and demonstrating reliability can lead to promotions and opportunities for growth.

There are always stumbling blocks along the way that challenge our efforts, but it is our ability to face them that is determined by our actions. We learn more through adversity for we build resilience and that mental toughness ensures success if we preserve it. We grow stronger and develop the capacity to face even greater challenges if we have faith in our efforts and have the willingness to hand over all to our Higher Power who I prefer to call God.

Action always speaks louder than words, but words have the power to inspire those around us and in turn our mantra for daily living into action if we are committed to our course. When we lead by example, showing dedication, integrity, and a commitment to our values, we become role models for others. Our actions can ignite the spark of motivation in those who look up to us.

Let us not forget that despite overwhelming feelings that may bring on fear, if we individually and collectively have the courage of our convictions and act on them we can achieve great things. Whether we're making a conscious effort to be kinder, pursuing personal growth, building relationships, contributing to social causes, or excelling in our career choices, our actions shape our world in profound ways.

In the words of D. Rajdeep: "Every choice we make, every word we speak, and every action we take leaves an imprint on the world around us. So, let's embrace the power of our actions, knowing that they have the potential to create positive change, inspire others, and shape a brighter future for all. As individuals, we can make a difference, and together, we can create a world that reflects the best of our collective humanity."

And you may never know, one day someone may write about you, for the deeds you do for the betterment of 'to whom it may concern.'

About the Author

Doug McPhillips, poet, singer, songwriter, and author, commenced his journey of discovery over a decade ago after life-changing experiences.

The many tracks he has traversed through the Northern Hemisphere and down under in Australia and New Zealand have resulted in the facts and fiction of this novel. Doug has written twenty books in all and recorded three albums of songs inspired by his journeys.

Doug is an adventurer who divides his time between family and friends, his creative pursuits, and those who benefit most from his efforts and experience.

Check out www.caminoway.com.au website for more about this author.

Reference Material

Selected Writings - Thomas Aquinas (Author)-Penguin 1989.

Albatross Book of Verse-J.R. Foreman-Collins-1966.

Speeches That Changed The World-Quercus Publishers-2005

Great Australian Speeches- Pamela Robson-Murdock-2009

Masters at My Table-Doug McPhillips-IngramSpark- 2019.

The Power of Active Shapes-D. Rajdeep- Academia-2023.

Reference material from Google Research- Authors Unknown.

www.ingramcontent.com/pod-product-compliance
Lightning Source LLC
Chambersburg PA
CBHW072013290426
44109CB00018B/2225